Dreams

A *Window* to the Unseen

ISBN-978-1-950252-13-8

Dreams

A *Window* to the Unseen

By Summer McClellan

Other Books by Summer McClellan

The Impossible Marriage

What Can I Do for God?

Satan Has No Power Over You

Faith, What is It?

Jesus is Our Example

Passing the Tests of Life

Grace, What is It?

Created in His Image

Light and Darkness

Broken Hearts

Love, What is It?

Dedicated to,

Laurielle Mc Clellan,

Jonathan Davila,
and

Steve Steinbeck

You three are a mother in law's dream come true.

Table of Contents

Volume Three
Symbols

For God may speak in one way, or in another, Yet man does not perceive it. In a dream, in a vision of the night, When deep sleep falls upon men, While slumbering in their beds, Then He opens the ears of men, And seals their instruction. In order to turn man from his deed, And conceal pride from man, He keeps back his soul from the Pit, And his life from perishing by the sword. Job 33:14-18

Introduction

Dreams have played an important role in my life. I was a person who did not know herself. In fact, I was sure I had no personality at all. I stumbled through life broken. It was confusing because it was all I knew. No one seemed to realize how broken I was but, as I entered my early teens, it became more evident. I would have destroyed myself if the Lord had not rescued me, and I almost did. He rescued me when I was fourteen years old. He became my everything.

But still I was broken. It was like a bomb went off in my personality and destroyed the person who was supposed to be there. It is hard to go through life and function and act normal, when inside you, you have been chopped up into little pieces. How do little pieces get up and live?

Only God knew the devastation inside of me. I did not know myself. I know I just lived in constant fear and confusion. Life was something to be endured. But God opened a window to the unseen things inside of me. He used my dreams. I did not know the mysteries they held at first, but over time God, through my dreams showed me what was inside of me and began to put the pieces back together.

God has changed my life through my dreams. I may have looked normal on the outside, but inside was a world no one knew, not even myself. God had been giving me the answers I had needed all along, they were hidden right there in plain sight. They were in my dreams.

Volume 1

Summer's Story

Chapter One

Life and Death

We were swimming at a nearby lake. It was a gorgeous spot. It was a small lake surrounded by woods. It was small enough that I could swim across it in about ten minutes, and I often did. It had at one time been a camp and now it had been given to the county for a park. Ever since we discovered this beautiful place it had become our favorite swimming spot. The only bad thing about it was there had been several drownings here. Unexplained drownings, and for that reason I was always extra careful when we swam here.

All five of my grandchildren were here this day, my son, James and his two children, Kellan aged eight, his daughter Mikaila aged six. Also, my daughter, Joy was here with her three, David aged four, Frankie three, and Hailey two. Because my five grandchildren were there, I barely noticed the other people swimming that day. I knew there were a group of teenagers, several boys and girls about eighteen years old or so, but I barely saw them because about every two minutes I was doing a head check on my five grandchildren. I wanted to be sure they were okay.

Kellan and Mikaila were on an inner tube with their dad, out kind of deep. David was swimming all over, he was an excellent swimmer even at age four. There was Frankie and Hailey splashing near shore. A minute or so later I would start again, checking all five. It was taking all my concentration. I was standing near shore on my watch when suddenly I noticed a few feet away from me one of the teenagers was dragging his friend out of the water the best he could.

I gasped, his friend, a muscular young man about nineteen had turned grey. He looked dead. His friend, a big fellow, dragged him half out of the water and could get his dead weight no further. He stopped and yelled, "Does anyone know CPR!"

I was frozen in disbelief. I had never seen anyone drown before. My daughter, Joy who was standing a few feet from me yelled back, "My mom does she works for the hospital!"

"Oh, that is me," I realized. I had trained for CPR every few years for my job as a home health aide. I snapped out of it and knelt down in the ankle-deep water and began rescue breathing. The young man's friend began the heart compressions.

Even though in the peripheral, I realized a crowd had gathered and were watching us intently, my total attention was focused on this young man. My eyes stayed intently on his face. He became the most important thing in the world to me. I was not going to let this beautiful young man slip into an eternity without Jesus. I realized, I am a child of God, I will not let the devil take him, I will not let him die. In those moments I made up my mind if all my years as a Christian meant anything, it meant I had right standing with God and this young man was not going to be lost on my watch. I breathed for him and between every breath I called out to Jesus with all my might.

Breath

"Jesus! Jesus! Jesus!"

Breath.

"JESUS! JESUS! JESUS!"

I could hear my daughter Joy in the background, but I did not see her because my eyes were glued to his face. I heard Joy call 911 for help. Thank the Lord that she had brought her phone to the beach. Then she began to call out to Jesus also. Together we called between every breath, "JESUS! JESUS! JESUS!"

The young man threw up. It went in my mouth and all down the front of my bathing suit. I spit it out and continued. The color was returning to his face. He took in a deep breath on his own. For a minute I thought it was over but again he turned blue. I kept breathing for him and calling out to Jesus. Over and over, he threw up. I was covered with emesis. I really didn't care. In that moment this young man was my child. He was the most important thing in the world to me and I wasn't going to let him die.

Somewhere in this time which was probably only fifteen minutes or so I looked up. I saw in the crowd my four-year-old grandson David.

"Oh no," I thought, "How will this affect him?"

I found out later my son had gotten the other four children and took them away so they wouldn't see what he thought they were too young to see, but David had been left behind and watched, {God was in this.}

The young man took one more breath on his own but that was all. Soon the paramedics arrived with an AED to begin shock treatments to his heart. They shooed us away. I ran to my car; I had to get alone and pray.

"Death, I rebuke you!" I screamed.

I heard a voice. It said, "It is too late."

"No, it is not too late!" I screamed again thinking it may be the enemy trying to deter me. "He will not die on my watch!"

I drove home praying at the top of my lungs. I jumped in the shower but never stopped praying. I was absolutely exhausted. Finally, I called my prayer partner

Rhonda to help me pray. She said, "I feel peace. I think everything is going to be okay." I was sure the young man would live but I did not know.

I fell asleep that night and had a vivid dream.

I dreamt I was watching two giant birds fight. One was a giant vulture, and one was a huge bald eagle. The vulture was defeated and fell, the giant bald eagle won. He landed. I looked at him with awe. He was a magnificent creature, absolutely huge with golden eyes. He thrilled and terrified me at the same time.

The scene was a balcony bathed in light with a circle of trees and a nature area below it. The eagle had landed in this treed area. I looked down and saw my grandson Franklin there. As beautiful as this eagle was, I knew he could easily hurt my grandson. I felt dread realizing my grandson was in harm's way. I called to my husband who is not afraid of animals like I am. He was standing on the balcony. The balcony overlooked the whole scene.

"Jim, Jim!" I called my husband desperately. "Hurry, kill it, you have to kill it." I knew Frankie was in danger.

Jim didn't hurry. He slowly walked down from the balcony and stood next to me. I begged him to kill the eagle. I could feel Frankie's impending doom.

Jim said, "I can't. It is too beautiful." Then he walked back to the balcony.

In horror I watched as the eagle took Frankie's head in his mouth. I reached out and tried to pry it off Frankie's head. I grabbed the eagle's mouth and began wrestling it. He was so huge and so powerful I could not budge his mouth. I was eyeball to eyeball with this fierce creature with the golden eyes and wrestling with all my might, I could feel his giant beak in my hands when I woke up. My eyes immediately looked at the clock and the time was 5:58.

I woke up out of breath as if I had been wrestling. My first thought was, "Oh no, now Frankie needs prayer too. I'm worn out from praying so hard for the young man yesterday, now Frankie too."

That morning I had to go to work, but I was on pins and needles waiting to hear how the young man was doing. I was also shaken up from the vivid dream. I called Joy to find out if she had heard anything, we both wanted to know what happened to the boy.

As I pulled out of the driveway that morning, I got a shock. My husband loves eagles, and he has a big wooden eagle sitting at the end of our driveway. I looked at it as I passed. It had a golden eye; I had never noticed it before! It sent shivers down my spine as it brought the golden eye from the dream back to me. It felt surreal, the dream had been so real and now this wooden eagle in my driveway almost seemed alive.

That morning at work my patient let me turn on the news. The story from the beach was on television, but just that a young man had been taken to the hospital. They had no word on his condition. I was so hopeful that he would be fine. Just before the end of my shift, Joy called me, "Mom, she said in shock, "He died." Joy had been praying too, as hard as I was.

I was crushed.

I couldn't stop the tears. I had let this young man down.

I couldn't function. I somehow got through the rest of my shift and drove to my twin sister, Carol's house about five minutes away. I stumbled into her house heart broken and crying. I had let this beautiful young man down.

I wondered, maybe I hadn't prayed hard enough? My voice was still hoarse, and my throat still hurt from the day before. I had literally cried out to God with all my might! I fell into a chair grief stricken. As I sat there the dream from the night before came to mind.

Suddenly I knew what my dream meant! I was not dreaming about Franklin, my grandson. The dream was about this young man that drowned, and this dream was the answer!

I stopped crying. I was no longer sad but filled with joy, wonder and amazement. I had not let the young man down. The young man was in heaven. He was there. The answer was in the dream.

The dream meant this. The two giant birds I saw fighting were the two kinds of death. The vulture was evil he was a spirit of death to take someone to hell, the eagle was death also, but good, he was there to take someone to heaven. There was a struggle over this young man's soul, but the great eagle won the fight, the young man went to heaven.

Jim, my husband, stood for Jesus. I called out to Jesus, {Jim.} I asked Him to kill the eagle, but He said it was too beautiful. This is straight out of scripture, **Psalms 116:15 Precious in the sight of the Lord is the death of His saints.** The reason the boy was Franklin in the dream was because of Franklin's name, it means free man. This young man was set free. And my wrestling with the eagle was me wrestling with the spirit of death, but it was not to be because it was this young man's time, and he is with the Lord!

I sat there in awe of the peace I felt. A peace that came from a God given dream.

But there is more. This young man's death had an impact on my four-year-old grandson David. That night at bedtime David said to his mother, "Mommy that boy died."

"Yes," Joy responded.

"Mommy, I want to pray."

David gave his heart to the Lord that night. What he observed made him realize about life and death and that he needed Jesus to face death. David is twelve years old now and his faith in God is still the most important thing to him.

This dream spoke volumes to me. There was a struggle over this boy's soul, but God won. He is in heaven with God and God let me know that through a dream.

I had called out to Jesus with all my might, and He hadn't failed me. He was doing what was best for everyone.

God's answer was in my dream. I have had many answers in my life come to me through dreams. Well let's go to the beginning.

Chapter Two

The Beginning

A phrase I have heard my whole life is, "it was only a dream." In other words, dreams aren't real, there is nothing to them. And that is what I thought dreams were, something insignificant. My childhood had been plagued by nightmares and I was actually afraid to dream because of the nightmares that caused me to wake up shaking in fear or crying uncontrollably.

I have since learned that nothing could be further from the truth. Dreams are something very real, they are a window to the unseen. They can show us about ourselves, the mysteries in our subconscious. The things we don't know about ourselves. They can warn us of what is coming. They can give us better perspective and they guide us.

God speaks to us in dreams. He guides us in

dreams. He warns us through dreams. And He can even correct us through dreams. I have found answers through dreams. I am no longer afraid to dream. I love dreams, they fascinate me. I love dreams, because I love to hear from God, and also dreams in their symbolic language, are mysteries, a mystery to solve.

Dreams have played an important role in my life and in many ways have changed my life. Finding out that dreams were more than just nonsense, began when I was a teenager. Before I went to bed one night, I felt that God told me I was going to have a dream that night, and He wanted me to pay attention to it.

I did, and this is what I dreamt. *I dreamt I was upstairs in my bedroom looking out the window. Outside were vicious black dogs. They were barking at me ferociously. I was so afraid that I was shaking even though I was upstairs in my room and my dad was fending off the dogs. My dad was outside standing in front of the house facing the dogs, and he was not afraid.*

The scene changed. My dad was with me in my bedroom. He was pointing out to me that I had an infection. It was a pimple on my face. He said it looks small, but it is really deep, then he pulled it out it was a huge thing with deep root.

To understand any dream, you have to look at the life of the dreamer and what they are going through. At this time in my life, I had been a Christian a little more than a year. I was going through demonic attacks that had begun shortly after I became a Christian. [I wrote more about this in my book, *Satan Has No Power over You.*] Actually, the trouble had even started before I was saved. I would hear knocking on the walls and things would disappear and then later reappear. After I became a Christian the attacks continued. My dad who had also become a Christian, would pray for me. Although I was intimidated by the devil, my dad was not. Knowing what was going on in my life makes this dream easier to understand. The big, black, vicious dogs represented the demonic attack.

The next day after the dream my dad asked to talk to me. He came in my room and sat me down. He explained to me how fear had gotten a hold in my life and that it may seem like a little thing, but it was a big thing. The situation was surprisingly like my dream, only in my dream the Lord was using a picture of infection to give further meaning to the words my dad was saying to me. It gave the whole message further depth. Then the next day at church, the pastor's whole sermon was on fear and sounded surprisingly like my dad's talk.

This was my first big lesson in interpreting a dream. The Lord made it very easy. The meaning to the dream was obvious. The black dogs were the demons that were attacking me. I was terrified even though my dad was standing between me and the dogs. My dad came in and talked to me just as he had in the dream. He pointed out that fear had gotten a hold in my life and the infection was deep. Then God even confirmed the message through the sermon the next day at church. I was so amazed to have had a dream from God and to know what it meant. God was dealing with me about fear. The whole thing was very fascinating.

But I thought it was a onetime event. After this experience with a dream, I went right back to ignoring my dreams thinking that if I were to have another dream that meant something, God would tell me again. So, my dreams went back on the shelf. I didn't pay attention to them. I wasn't very comfortable with dreams because my childhood had been plagued by nightmares.

Chapter Three

Nightmares

My childhood was plagued by nightmares. I mean my very early childhood. I had four dreams that I can remember having over and over. One was about a lady who I called the lady in the safari suit. That is what I called her when I would try to convey the dream to my twin sister, Carol, to whom I told everything. *The lady in the safari suit wore a tan dress and a safari hat. She always did the same thing just in different settings. She cut my mom, my twin sister and I, up into little pieces. After she cut us up, I would still be alive, but I was laying on the ground in little pieces.*

One of those settings, I called a bullfighter ring. I was little and I had seen a bullfighter ring in cartoons, but it wasn't really a bullfighter ring. I was just too little to know what it was. It was a Roman coliseum. The coliseum was just outside my mother's bedroom and the lady in the safari suit was there in front of a huge crowd as she cut us up in pieces. There were many places she would cut us up.

One time she cut us up in my grandmother's back yard.

Another of my series of nightmares was equally as terrifying, although it doesn't seem so terrifying. *I would be looking through a closet and as I looked through it, I would find a door in the back of the closet. I knew something horrible was behind that door. I would be so terrified I would wake up shaking every time. As soon as I would see that door, the choking, blinding, fear would overwhelm me. This dream plagued me for years.*

Then the third dream that I had frequently was of falling. *I would be swinging on a swing or doing some activity and suddenly I would feel this horrible feeling coming on and I would fall. I would hit hard, and my heart would beat out of my chest.* I would wake up breathless.

The fourth dream I had was of a great loss. *I would be playing a card game, or some game and I would lose. The loss I felt was so great I would wake up crying uncontrollably.*

Why would a tiny child have such miserable dreams?

Again, the answer is knowing what was going on in my life. Part of which I didn't even know myself, until much later in my life when the Lord directed me to ask my mother questions about my beginning. My mom had never explained to my sister and I why things were the way they were.

Dreams are a window into the unseen and my

unseen held many awful secrets of abuse and rejection which showed up in the form of nightmares. My sister and I had a very rough start in life.

My sister, Carol and I were born to a single teenaged mother. We did not know the story until we were in our thirties and God instructed me to ask my mother about it. My mother's parents were old enough to be her grandparents. They were born in the late 1800's. My mom lived a very sheltered life, and she was no match for the slick traveling salesman that came to town and began dating her. He was older than she was and drove a fancy car and took her to fancy restaurants. When she found out she was pregnant her parents were horrified. They sat this man down and said he had to marry their daughter and he agreed.

After a wedding shower given to mom by her dear friends, she and her fiancé packed up and left for his hometown. He had said they would get married there. My mother's happiness soon turned to horror when they arrived at his home. She found out he already had a wife and three children. She was left with nowhere to go. Her parents would not let her return. She could not even keep their name. She was staying in a camper in his yard until mom's married brother took her in, just before we were born.

Mom's parents thoroughly rejected her but that was before I had the ability to remember. They came around after we were born so I had no idea of the rejection we received from them early on. My grandparents were my favorite people in the whole world.

My sister and I got off to a rocky start and it got even rockier. My mom was proposed to by a man who did not want to go to Vietnam. He was abusive and a pedophile. Those were dark days, the few memories I had of him were not good. Even after my mom divorced him our lives were chaotic. Our mom had to work, and we were always with babysitters.

Because of the horror of my experience with babysitters I have never left my children with babysitters. I would have starved to death first. Jim and I lived on what he could earn for many years and when the time came that I had to work, I had a paper route. I worked in the middle of the night. And if I had to, I could bring the kids with me.

I don't want to get into abuse too much because this is a book on dreams. But I want you to understand why my childhood dreams were nightmares. There was so much trauma hidden in my past. Much of it I was even too little to remember. The nightmares were there for a reason. We are complex beings, we humans; I will get into that in a later chapter. Our pasts are still alive inside of us and need to be dealt with and that was showing up in my dreams. From my earliest memories of dreams, they were nightmares.

Chapter Four

Dreams Revealed

"We both had dreams," they answered, "But there is no one to interpret them." Then Joseph said to them, "Do not interpretations belong to God? Tell me your dreams." Genesis 40:8

When I was in my early twenties, I got a hold of the book by Herman Riffel called, *Dreams God Neglected Gift.* I love to read. I was reading my way through our church library, which was huge, when I came across this book.

The book is about a man, Herman, a minister that realizes God is speaking to him in his dreams. The book follows his journey of dream interpretation. At one point he left his church to study dream interpretation at Jung Institute and then dream interpretation became his ministry.

Herman Riffel's book was the only book I could find at that point on dreams. [Now, there are many books available on dreams, and I have tried to read them all.] Reading that book was life changing for me. I finally realized that dreams were not just dreams. They had meaning. I realized I had been missing important messages. Although I had a dream or two, I knew were from God, I thought that was a very rare thing and I ignored my dreams.

When I read that book, I thought back to my childhood nightmares which at that point hadn't stopped and I realized they meant something. I thought about my worse dream of all, the one that scared me the most and I had countless times. The dream where I am going through the closet, and I get to the back of the closet and there is a door. When I see this door, the fear becomes overwhelming, and I wake up in terror. I know something horrible is behind that door.

I realized this was real and I needed to find out what was behind that door. I had two toddlers at the time, Jamie my son who was three and Lonna my daughter who was one. I waited until I put them down for their afternoon nap and I decided I was going to open that door. I closed my eyes and went to the back of the closet and opened it. I wasn't prepared for what happened next.

I was in my crib, in the dark, I think I was about two. I was not an adult, remembering being two, I was two. There was a man standing next to the crib in the dark. I was feeling the strongest feeling of terror that I had ever felt in my life. I knew what was about to happen, but I couldn't face it. I knew the man was the abusive stepfather I had when I was very little. But now he was bigger than life and looming over me. And there it was that same fear from my nightmare. It was also the same fear I have had my whole life, it seemed to always be present but not this strong, a terrifying paralyzing fear.

I opened my eyes and bolted for my children. I was so scared that I ran and held them. I needed another human being.

It was no wonder that dream held so much fear. Locked away inside me was a memory that was too painful for me to handle, but it was something I needed to deal with. I couldn't bear to open that door again, at least not alone.

About a year and a half later the Lord led me to the counselor that He had handpicked to help me through that memory. It was a divine appointment. The minute I stepped into her office the Lord told her I had been molested as a child. When I told her the dream and we prayed, the memory unlocked, and the Lord was able to heal me. I felt like a new person afterwards. The terror behind the door was dealt with. It couldn't torment me anymore. The dream I had my whole life never returned.

After reading Herman's book I immediately understood many dreams. My dreams were dealing with my broken personality and my many inner unbalances. The window to the unseen inside of me was revealing what God wanted me to deal with.

I dreamt of a large hotel that was totally in shambles. A huge ugly vine had grown through all the walls and the walls had buckled and folded. The ugly vine had grown through every room but one at the very top of the hotel. I was living in that one room and had all my possessions in there. I was very crowded.

The large hotel was my personality, and the ugly vine was fear. The fear had almost totally destroyed my personality and I was living in the very small part that was left.

I dreamt a very kind lady that I knew from our church was angry and she plopped herself down on my mother's lap.

The dream was about the compassionate part of me. I am a very compassionate person, but my compassion was out of balance, it would overtake my reason.

I would dream I was screaming and swearing at a family member who caused me pain.

This dream was just showing me I had suppressed rage. I couldn't express my feelings in real life.

I dreamt I was standing in church worshipping in a sequin gown like a movie star.

On top of all my other faults, I was very self-centered. I would not have admitted that in a million years, but it slapped me in the face in a dream.

I dreamt I was attracted to a boy from my old neighborhood that I liked before I got saved, He was the neighborhood bad boy.

This dream would come around every once in a while, and it stood for my old sin nature. I was courting it again! I knew I was heading the wrong direction when I would have this dream.

I dreamt my husband and I were sitting at a table, on a plate in front of Jim was a slice of an onion, on a plate in front of me was a green onion.

I had no idea, until I had this dream that oral sex was displeasing to the Lord. There was even a popular Christian book on marriage going around at the time which said to do whatever your husband wanted you to. I learned it was wrong in from this dream and never did that again.

I would dream over and over that I was chewing gum and it didn't taste good and I would try to get it out of my mouth, and it kept sticking to my teeth and I couldn't get rid of it.

Have you ever talked too much, and you know you are saying things you shouldn't and the more you try to stop the more you talk? That was a real problem of mine, which is why I had this dream so many times.

God was unveiling to me things I needed to deal with in my dreams. I knew I was broken but I did not know how to get fixed. Those answers were coming to me in my dreams. But that wasn't all. God helped me to see me husband through His eyes, through my dreams.

Chapter Five

The Giants and Tornadoes

God has helped with my marriage, through the years, through my dreams. I wrote my whole story in my book, *The Impossible Marriage.* You already know that I had a troubled childhood, but mine was nothing compared to my husband, Jim's childhood.

Jim suffered rejection from the womb also. Jim's childhood was equally devastating. His parents were divorced soon after Jim was born, and Jim barely knew his father until just before he died. Jim was in trouble from his earliest memories. His mother dealt with him by keeping him locked up in the closet. When he became school age he didn't go. He'd sneak out most days and he wandered the streets. After ninth grade, he never went back.

In my childhood the abuse stopped, in my husband's life the abuse never stopped. He was stabbed by an older brother and almost died. He was knocked unconscious when an older sister hit him in the head with a brick. He was clobbered by an axe. His body is covered with scars. He also suffered much sexual abuse and incest. But I think some of his deepest scars are from rejection and being told he was worthless.

Jim fought back. He was at war with the world and constantly in trouble. His first felony was before the age of fourteen. I found that out when I saw his record one time. Jim's second home was the juvenile hall. As he grew older, he spent time in the county jail and the House of Correction. Eventually at age 23 Jim got sent to prison for 3- 15 years.

When I met Jim, he was twenty-seven years old, and he had spent a good part of his childhood and almost all of his life in some sort of jail prison or corrective program. There was a good reason for this. Jim was wild. He was so wild; he was always kept in maximum security. And when he was out on parole, he would get back in trouble and be locked up again soon. It was on Jim's second parole that we met. Actually, my parents met Jim first.

A man named. Frank, from our church, was sent to prison and my parents wrote to him. Jim approached Frank, knowing he was also a Christian, and asked Frank if he knew anyone that he could write to. Jim was very lonely and had no contact with the outside world. Once Jim wrote to my parents, they wrote him back and visited him. After Jim was paroled, they realized Jim wasn't doing well. They decided to go get him and bring him to our house to help him.

I was with my parents when they went to get him. As troubled as Jim was, Jim is also the warmest person I have ever met. When he got in the car with us that day and rode in the back seat with me, I was so uncomfortable. I slid over and turned toward the door on my side of the car. I suddenly got interested in looking out the window. When Jim got in the car that day, he was nobody to me and I wasn't interested in talking to him. When we got out of the car, a few hours later, I was totally smitten with him. He was the most important person in the world to me and would be for the rest of my life.

All my life I had felt like a non-person. I knew I didn't have a personality. I was not happy. I had no feelings, and I wondered why. In just a few minutes, Jim managed to touch the me that I did not know existed.

He was ten, almost eleven years older than me. I didn't care, I needed him.

He was an ex-convict who had been locked up since he was a teenager and couldn't function in the outside world. He was constantly in trouble and had been since the day he was born. And it wouldn't be long until he would be locked up again and again and again.

I didn't care. I needed him. I was hooked on him. I was smitten. I followed him around constantly. I was attached to him by a deep inner need that I did not understand myself and it made no sense to anyone else I knew or that knew me. I just needed him.

We have been married close to forty years now. It has been hard, very, very, very hard. I still need him. I still follow him. Jim tells people, "I patted her on the head, and she's been following me ever since."

If you were to look at the two of us, we might have looked normal, but we weren't. I was a non-person who had never developed a personality and I was full of fear and very self- centered. Jim was schizophrenic. He had several personalities, which were demonic, and they were stronger than his real personality.

Of course, I did not understand any of that then. I just knew things were very wrong and never seemed to be alright for very long. But God had brought us together and that I knew for sure, although no one else knew it. I have been told by countless, well-meaning people that I married out of God's will.

My dreams played a huge role in my marriage surviving. Jim was so angry and explosive and out of control, and I was so fearful and self-centered. I had to see things from God's perspective. God accomplished that through my dreams. I was so sure I was an abused wife, but God had to get me to see the unseen.

I remember one day early in our marriage, although we did have two children by this time, that I took my two children and fled to my sister's house. Jim could be like a wild beast. He could tear up everything in his path and scream for hours. Jim did not hit me or beat me. His anger was not directed at me, although he always felt beneath me and would sneer, "You think you're so holy." But still, he would terrify me. This night he had been drinking and he was in a rage. I took the kids and escaped. Feeling safe at my sister's, I told her and my brother-in-law how awful Jim was acting. Later when Jim fell asleep on the couch, the kids and I went home and went to bed. That night I had a dream.

I dreamt I was standing in a house looking out the window and there were four giants outside. They were attacking Jim. Jim was no match for them. Jim was lying on the street in a pool of blood. "Look at him!" I said pointing at Jim critically like I was disgusted with him. Suddenly I realized how hurt he was. The giants were throwing huge rocks at him, and he was very wounded. I felt compassion on him, so I let him in the house. This angered the giants when I let Jim in the house, so they broke into the house and began to attack me.

I recognized my behavior from the dream. Just as I had gone to my sister's house and criticized and pointed my finger at Jim, so to speak, I was doing the same thing in the dream. But the dream showed me a whole new perspective. I wasn't the one being hurt, Jim was. He had four big enemies, and he was their target. When I showed Jim love, they attacked me too. But only to get me to stop helping Jim. They hated me for that.

God had gotten me through to me, through this dream, to realize something. These four giants in the dream were demonic strongholds within Jim. They were his enemies. Jim was no match for them. And the most important thing I learned is that Jim was their target, not me. That Jim was the direct target, and he was in much greater pain than I was, even though my pain was very great. God also accomplished something else through this dream, or I should say began to start accomplishing something else. I was angry with Jim, for the drinking and the abuse. I was very angry. So, angry, I wanted to criticize him and hurt him, and many times I did. But what God was showing me was that my anger was to be directed at the giants, not Jim. They were the real enemies. Yes, it looked like Jim, because they were inside of Jim, but it was not Jim. The way for me to beat the giants was to love and forgive Jim. I hated those giants.

God had showed me also that in Jim's lifetime he had never really been loved by anyone until he met my parents. And yet he was using all the love he had. Even though Jim looked like a horrible failure and a drunk, he was pleasing God. Those enraged giants wanted Jim to beat me. I could feel the violence under the surface. The verbal abuse was terrible. The rage was terrible, but he never actually hit me. Jim was using all the love he had.

This was not an easy lesson and many times I failed miserably. I went through an angry period for a while where I would just lose it and try to hurt Jim, either physically or emotionally. I would actually get frustrated because he is so strong, and I would try to hit him or kick him where it hurts. Then when my anger would subside, I will be so ashamed of myself. God had to just stop me. He told me, "When you are angry with Jim and you want to hurt him, you do not have to do anything, remember that you do not have to do anything, he is already hurting."

That was another life-changing point for me. I would stop and think he is already hurting, and I never wanted to hurt him again.

But those giants were in my dreams for years, to keep my focus on my real enemies. And in time Jim became stronger until finally there was only one giant left. Jim still is struggling with that last giant. It has to do with addiction.

Giants weren't the only thing that reappeared over and over in my dreams, there were also the tornadoes. The tornadoes also were inside of Jim. When they would hit, all hell would break loose in our lives. The tornadoes were a result of the different personalities within Jim warring for control and the pressure in him would build and build. Usually, to deal with the invisible pressure that only he was feeling he would have to drink for any relief, and what we his family saw was an angry out of control drunken man.

God always warned me when a storm in Jim was

coming. I always dreamed of a tornado first. Although I hated those tornadoes at least I was prepared as much as I could be because I knew they were coming.

God was communicating with me through my dreams. He was helping me to understand things and see things through His eyes. Through my dreams God was helping me to overcome. God was helping me in so many ways through my dreams, not only with my past, but also with my marriage. He was teaching me and helping me, and it was coming through my dreams.

Volume 2

Interpreting Dreams

In this section we will look at interpreting dreams. To help understand each dream we look at I will give some background as to what circumstances were surrounding me before each dream. It is my hope that sharing my stories and what I have learned will help you begin to interpret your own dreams. Here we go.

Chapter Six

Many Different Kinds of Dreams

There are many different types of dreams. It is helpful to classify each dream. It helps us to understand it. The different types of dreams each have a different purpose. Here are some of the different types of dreams.

Guidance Dreams

One thing that has always been scary to me has been buying a car. We have never had enough income to be able to afford a car payment so we have always bought old cars with whatever cash we could scrounge up. Once we bought a car that lasted one day. It was such a lemon. From that time on, I learned to pray and pray before buying a car.

For the last eighteen years I have worked on my

job as a home health aide. I have to drive from house to house to visit patients. So, I need to have a decent car because I drive so much for my job. That has made my car situation even more serious.

Well, I thought the car I had was going to last me a few more years, so I wasn't too concerned that I had no money saved up for a car. Our shed in our backyard had totally rotted out. We were saving to replace it and had 1500 dollars and we were about to rebuild it when my car broke down. The mechanic told me the repair cost so much that it exceeded the value of the car. He advised me not to fix it. Suddenly I needed a car and all I had was the money for the shed. We realized that the shed would have to wait and started looking for a car. The only problem was there wasn't anything I could find for that price.

Well, it just so happened my son, Jay, had put a car in my driveway he had bought for cheap, just to resell. The problem was he hadn't driven it first. The thing drove very rough and made a deafening sound when you drove it. I wondered what he was going to do with it. In the middle of this situation, I had a dream.

I dreamt I was in an old house that we used to live in. The floor was damaged. My brother-in-law Walter who is a carpenter came to assess the damage. The floor was covered in brown carpet, {not the real color of the carpet in that house}. Walter examined the floor and then

37

announced, "This is fixable."

I woke up and wondered, "What in the world did that dream mean?" Then I just forgot about it.

Jim and I went to see our mechanic, Tim, that day because he often has a fixed-up car to sell. But he didn't have anything we could afford. Jim told Tim about the car Jay had bought but said, "It is so bad we don't even dare drive it over here." Our mechanic told us, "Go get it."

So, we brought it there even though I thought it was going to explode. Tim looked at the car and said, "This is fixable."

All of a sudden, I thought of the dream. The car was brown like the carpet in the dream. My brother-in-law, in the dream, stood for an expert in his field, like Tim the car expert. I knew the dream meant this was the car for me. It was guidance. My son gave me the car, and Tim, the mechanic, was able to fix it for the money we had saved up for the shed. I loved that car! It was all wheel drive and it drove wonderful in the winter. It was a real blessing. It was wonderful to know exactly what to do because the guidance came in a dream. I love guidance dreams!

Warning Dreams

A close friend of our pastor, had a dream *that he was boating with his family when the boat turned over and one of his daughter's drowned.* She took it upon herself to fervently pray for protection over him and his family. She also told him the dream. Well, the dream happened. They were boating, and they had the same accident that was described to him in the dream, but the outcome was different. His daughter was rescued and didn't drown. The warning dream was heeded. This time the answer was prayer, and this woman's prayers saved the daughter of our pastor.

Sometimes a different action may be required. I had a warning dream about my patient, Myra. I took care of Myra for over twelve years. Every time something major happened in her life I would dream about it first. This time I had a warning dream.

I dreamt she was in bed, and I heard a thud and turned around. I didn't see her, but I saw a circle of blood on the floor, and I thought, "Uh oh. This is bad."

At this time, she was planning a trip. She wanted me and another aide to take her for a couple of days to her hometown. I knew this dream was a warning that her health could not take it. When my supervisor called me to discuss us going, I just told her I wouldn't do it, because I did not think she was healthy enough.

I have learned to trust the warnings from God in my dreams. I actually would have loved to go, because I would have earned tons of overtime, and it would have been fun. But instead, I heeded the dream.

Warning dreams are very common. All my tornado dreams were warning dreams. Although they were not something I could pray away, the Lord let me know what was coming, so that I could be as ready as possible.

Cleansing Dreams

Sometimes we are exposed to something gross. This may show up in our dreams as a purging it from our system. One time I was at a patient's house, for my job as a home health aide. I was exposed to an awful movie that he was watching while I was caring for him. It gave me a horrible feeling. I had a dream that night.

I dreamt I was with my patient, and I had a clean bowl. He put a slimy creature in my clean bowl.

Of course, the dream was referring to the movie I was exposed to. It had defiled me. When I woke up the Lord told me I had to stop working on the book I was writing for a few weeks. I stopped writing until He told me it was okay again. I had to wait because my soul was defiled.

Other times when I have seen something foul during the day it may show up in my dream that night. I realize it is a way of cleansing my soul.

Literal Dreams

I remember the first time I had a literal dream I was about sixteen years old.

I dreamt I was standing at my bedroom window looking out at the pine forest that lined our front yard. It was winter and it was snowing snowballs. It wasn't snowflakes, it was snowballs. They were so big that plopped on the ground when they landed. It was a beautiful sight, and I woke up amazed.

This was back in my, "it's just only a dream" mentality. It was after my first dream God had told me I was going to have, the dream about the big black dogs, and my dad sat me down the next day and talked about fear. But it was several years before I had read Herman Riffle's book on dreams and started taking dreams seriously.

Well, a few weeks later I was standing looking out of my bedroom window and I saw the exact same sight I saw in my dream. I saw huge snowballs falling and plopping on the ground. What I could see in real life, that I could not see in the dream was that there was so much snow in the trees that a wind came up and disturbed it, making it look like it was snowing snowballs. The scene was identical to the dream. I stood there looking out and gasped, in amazement. Partly at the sight and partly because I had dreamed this very thing a few weeks beforehand. I had always wondered why I dreamed that; it was a beautiful sight but what did it mean? I realize now, years later in hindsight, that God was trying to get me to take dreams seriously. The dream was His way of showing me to pay attention to my dreams, but it would be a few more years before I got the message.

Another literal dream I had was again about my patient, Myra.

I dreamt she was in the hospital and in a hospital bed. The orderly was caring for her and was in a hurry. He quickly flipped her over and she moaned in pain. In the dream, I yelled I was so angry at how brusquely he handled her. Her body was very stiff, and I always did things slowly and gently, so as not to cause her pain.

A week or so after the dream, Myra was in the hospital. The scene happened just exactly as I dreamed except it was a woman not a man who handled her roughly. I knew she appeared as a man in the dream because she "Manhandled her." Also, in real life I did not yell, but my emotions were yelling.

I do not know the purpose of this dream except that she never got better. The dreams increased, as she got closer to the end. My prayer partners and I prayed she would be ready to go when the time came.

I have had a few literal dreams but not too many.

Inner Healing Dreams

So many of my dreams have been inner healing dreams because I have needed so much inner healing. One dream I had that helped me immensely was after my parents' divorce. After their divorce I was devastated, and

I was having trouble dealing with it.

My parents got married when I was seven years old. It was the best thing that had ever happened to me. My life was scary and unpredictable before, I had suffered abuse. I hated always being left with babysitters because some had done awful things to me. When my mom met my new dad and married him, my nightmare was over. I had a dad and a stay-at-home mom. I finally felt safe for the first time in my life. I thought my parents would always be together. I could not deal with their divorce. It was too much for me, when I first found out they were getting a divorce, I became so depressed. I remember saying to myself, "Things will never be okay again."

I wasn't getting over it even after many months. I was angry and frustrated all the time. My emotions were on a constant roller coaster, and I cried myself to sleep every night.

My mom had immediately remarried, but she married such an awful man I knew it wouldn't last. It didn't. But I did not want my dad to meet anyone, because I was hoping as soon as my mom's marriage failed that they would get back together. That was all I wanted, for them to get back together. I resented anyone that came in my dad's life, because I had all my hopes fixed on them getting back together. I was feeling angry at my dad, not because I thought it was his fault. I blamed my mom, but because my mom's life was a mess and my dads wasn't. I was just struggling. Then I had this dream.

I dreamt I was floating behind a car with a man and lady in it. I was so happy behind the car, just floating there as they drove along. It was a feeling of absolute euphoria. All of a sudden, the car they were in turned and they were driving across railroad tracks. It gave me a sick feeling and I knew this was going to be bad. I had a feeling of absolute doom. A train passed on the driver's side, but it was so far off it was no threat. Then a train passed on the passenger side and came so close it almost hit the car. Suddenly a train hit right straight down the middle of the car. The impact was horrible. The man was thrown out of the car and ended up walking away, but the woman was wounded. I was left dazed and angry. I was so angry, I wanted to sue someone. But the woman was just to hurt to sue, so I tried to sue the man. When I did the man said, "I have already lost my house." I knew I could not sue him either. I knew the blame was with the owner of the train, but he was so evil I did not want to even think about him.

The scene changed, a phone rang, and I answered it. A woman's voice came on the phone and said, "Things will never be okay again."

This dream helped me to start healing. I saw in the dream that I was angry at my dad for no reason, just because I was so devastated. I knew that Satan was the owner of the train in the dream. He was the real one at fault. I also realized from the dream that it was not my mom's fault either. Their marriage had taken a wrong turn and was on the railroad tracks. The different trains were different people the devil was sending to try to break up their marriage, which was because they were on the railroad tracks. I am not exactly sure why.

I also knew what the phone call at the end of the dream meant. The Lord had taken that phrase from my own thoughts. It meant that they were not ever going to get back together. That was hard for me to take but once I realized that the Lord was not going to restore their marriage, ever, I stopped resenting every woman in my dad's life.

This dream could actually fit in three of our categories. It was a perspective dream. It gave me a different perspective on what happened. It was a guidance dream because it got me to give up a false hope that my parents were going to get back together. And it was an inner healing dream because it got me to stop blaming people and realize it was the devil's doing. It helped get over the anger and the grief I was feeling. It was the beginning of healing for me.

Prophetic Dreams

Prophetic dreams foretell the future. I have had some dreams years ago that tell of hard times ahead. As of yet only one of them has come to pass, but I will put them in for an example.

I dreamt I got up and looked out the window and as far as I could see was grey ash. Nothing was left standing.

I hope that dream doesn't come to pass, it seems to have been a nuclear bomb.

I dreamt that churches met in secret. I was in an apartment of a lady I had never met. There was nothing in the apartment but an old picnic table. We were having a prayer meeting and the Holy Spirit was moving mightily. I could see in the spirit and could see what was going on in other places. It was very powerful.

Another dream I had *was that I opened the grocery store ad, and the only thing in the ad was the produce section. Food was scarce.*

{I have to say this actually happened this week, during the coronavirus. When I had this dream the sale paper was about ten pages long. This week the sale paper was one page, only the produce.}

I just have these dreams on the shelf for now. They may be foretelling future events. I know I tend to be complacent. God had to wake me up with a dream. I remarked to my husband one day when he was talking about current events, "I am not afraid of what is coming." That night I had a dream. *I dreamt huge dark giants were coming from the East. They were marching across the land. I was terrified and wanted to escape. They came in dark whirlwinds. They came so quickly that I couldn't escape, so*

I just ran in the house and tried to hide.

I woke up and realized I was not ready for what was coming, whatever it was. It seemed supernatural and demonic. I called my sister and my daughter and told them the dream. We decided to start praying together for our family to be ready for what is coming on the earth. That was about five years ago. We still get together to pray, and the results have been amazing. We have had many wonderful answers to our prayers. The dream woke me up to pray!

Body Dreams

I have had many dreams that are dealing with a condition in my body. Such as when we were buying our first house. I had wanted a house for years. I was so focused on getting this house done so we could move in. I was painting and painting every day. But I was having trouble with my asthma, it was getting worse and worse. I was so focused on getting the house done I was ignoring it. Also, it is helpful to know that I had just graduated cosmetology school.

I dreamt I was bleaching my hair blonde, and I kept putting on more bleach, but it was too much and my hair damaged and broke off.

At first, I did not know the meaning of the dream,

but after praying about it I realized it was referring to my lungs and the painting. I was doing damage to my lungs. I had to stop painting. I told my husband the dream, and that my asthma was getting worse and worse, and he took over the painting. I needed the dream to help me realize that I needed to take care of the situation.

Another time I had a simple dream to alert me to a problem in my body.

I dreamt I had my pants on backwards, and the part that should have been on my bottom was on my front.

When I woke up, I realized I hadn't had a bowel movement in several days. I needed to take a laxative.

The Holy Spirit is concerned about our bodies and our health. He will reveal to us what our bodies need in our dreams.

One body dream I had was a direction to go to the doctor. For many years we did not have health insurance and I just trusted the Lord for my health. I would feel sick, but I would act well. I would ignore the symptoms and just trust God. Then even after we got health insurance I did not go to the doctor. It worked for many years. I would get a migraine headache and I could barely see, but I would go to work and begin work and it would disappear. One day I actually had stroke symptoms. I was talking to my daughter on the phone when I couldn't speak. I knew what I wanted to say, but I couldn't speak. Finally, I was able to say yes or no. Well, I went to work that day too. I could not afford to miss a day of work. While I was working, I got to feeling so bad I thought I was going to die, and then it just passed, and I was fine.

This is how I dealt with sickness until I had a dream.

I dreamt I was with a nurse getting an X-ray. The Xray showed two holes in my abdomen. The nurse told me, "You have to see a doctor."

I had been having pain in my abdomen, which I was ignoring as I always did. I knew the Lord was letting me know that now I was supposed to go to the doctor. When I did, I even told the doctor that the Lord told me in a dream to come. I ended up having to have surgery, in fact, it was a string of surgeries. I had many health problems. The Lord was changing the way we did things.

This was not a lack of faith on my part, but it was a change. I had never learned to eat right because of my low food budget. We rarely ate fruits and vegetables. During this time, I have had to operate my faith in another way. I had to spend money on healthy food and eat right.

Perspective Dreams

Sometimes I have dreams that don't seem to have the answer to a situation in my dream. It is just an image of what I am going through in symbolism. I am going to call those perspective dreams. They show what I am feeling and going through, but I get a different perspective on it.

One example of a perspective dream I had was

when I dreamt that I had an insatiable urge to drink alcohol. It was so strong I knew I could not control it unless I gave it all my attention and stopped everything else in my life. Also, I saw the urge was so strong that it was easier to just go into self-deception and accept it as normal. I had no idea before this dream the urge for alcohol could be so strong.

God was just showing me perspective in my dream. My husband was an alcoholic and I was critical of him because I wanted him to quit drinking!!!!!! God was showing me what he was up against and how much effort it would take.

Wake Up Dreams

Wake up dreams are intense dreams that wake you right up. Many times, after a wake up dream the issue that I was dreaming about happens the same day, but not always. Wake up dreams you want to pay attention to, and you want to pray about. They are something that needs to be dealt with.

Here is a wake-**up** dream I had recently. *I dreamt that a man walked in the house and went in the closet. I knew he was a pedophile. I called the police. In the room was little boy who was naked. {this little boy is a real boy I know who is a foster child. He was abused but he was the only child in the family who was abused. The abuser singled him out.} The man came out of the closet and was*

*walking slowly toward the door where my husband Jim
was standing. The man hit Jim and grabbed him by the
throat and was choking him. He was killing him; I was
pulling the man's hair trying to get him off Jim, but it didn't
even phase the man he was just too strong. I kept
wondering where the police were. I yelled to the kids who
were in the other room to call 911. I woke up struggling
with the man, my heart pounding!*

This dream is showing me my husband is wrestling
with a stronghold in his life and it is too strong for him. It is
also showing me where the stronghold is coming from, his
past. This dream is filled with symbols from his past. The
pedophile, {sexual abuse} the closet, {he was kept locked
in the closet,} and the little boy singled out for abuse but
not his siblings, {that was Jim's situation also}. This dream
is also showing me that I am not being effective either.

Jim, my husband, has C.O.P. D. which is similar to
emphysema. Jim knows he can't smoke anymore but this
addiction has been overpowering him and he coughs all
the time. As hard as he has been trying, he keeps having
trouble with the smoking issue and his health is suffering.
That is what this dream is about. It is showing me that the
stronghold is attached to the abuse in his past. It is
stronger than he is.

As of this writing this issue has not yet been
resolved. And also, as I am writing this, I am realizing that I
don't need to say another word to him about it, the dream

is showing me he is fighting his hardest. {Keep your mouth shut Summer} And I need more help praying this through. {911}

This was not a pleasant dream to have but it is necessary. Dreams are frequently showing us things that need dealing with and wake up dreams are serious issues.

Satanic Dreams

Some dreams do come from the devil. One time I was sound asleep, and the Holy Spirit woke me up immediately. There was a demonic being hovered over me focusing on my face. He had huge red eyes. As soon as this thing realized I was awake he immediately disappeared. It surprised me to be woken up so suddenly and it also surprised this evil thing, The Holy Spirit was protecting me by waking me up.

Also, I have had many times I feel I am wrestling with the devil in my sleep. I realized they were not dreams at all but demonic attacks. They always followed the same pattern, I would lay awake for hours unable to sleep, then I would begin to fall asleep but sense an evil presence. Then when I would try to move or wake up I could not. I would wrestle to wake up. I would feel a demon or hear him growling. Then, when I would wake up my neck would burn. It was horrible. I asked God how this happens, and I felt like He said," it attaches to your central nervous system." Even though I could not move a muscle when this happens as hard as I try, I can always pray in tongues, which is how I get free.

Spiritual Growth Dreams

Some dreams help us with our spiritual growth.

I dreamt I was walking with my dad when he suddenly grabbed his heart and fell down on the ground and died, his last words were, "Faith without works is dead."

This dream had nothing to do with my dad whatsoever or his health. My dad is the kind of person who gets things done. When I dream about my dad that is what he means. He stands for action. This dream was showing me where I was off spiritually. I thought I could just pray about everything and then wait for God to do it. God was showing me I needed to do my part. This dream was a turning point for me. I realized I needed more action when God revealed His plan to me. I can't just expect Him to drop everything in my lap.

Another spiritual growth dream ministered peace to me.

I dreamt of a friend of mine picked me up in a car. The car was red and shiny, but inside the interior was black and I noticed a little scuffed up. He picked me up and smiled at me and kissed me. I felt wonderful and we drove off together.

When I woke up from this dream the wonderful feeling stayed with me for days. The dream was about peace. The friend represented peace. The car represented my Christian walk. The fact that I was not perfect was represented by the scuffed up black interior of the car, but I was covered by the blood of Jesus, the shiny red outside of the car. The dream gave me such a wonderful feeling, and the feeling was peace. I had come into a place of peace and that was the purpose of the dream. Also, it gave me a hunger to stay in peace and seek peace.

Spiritual Warfare Dreams

A perfect example of a spiritual warfare dream is a dream my daughter Joy told me that she had. It foretold an attack on our church, that she was able to pray for.

In Joy's dream she found herself in an art gallery, but somehow, she knew this was Satan's art gallery. She stood in front of a picture which was hanging on the wall which was very beautiful. The picture was a farm scene. She was looking at a scene of a field full of beautiful sunflowers. But as she looked at the picture a bad feeling came over her. Suddenly in the middle of the picture a skeletal hand burst forth from the ground and started ripping out the sunflowers. Joy was horrified and woke up.

The field of sunflowers was our church. Satan attacked our church, as he does many churches, many members left. This dream was a call to pray for the church, which Joy did.

Fear Dreams

Some dreams are just showing us what we fear. After a close friend of my husband's died, I had this dream.

I dreamt I was standing on the front porch looking out when I heard a loud roar. My husband's car came racing out of the garage backwards and crashed into the garage across the street. Jim was lying on the ground. I went over and tried to revive him.

I believe this is a fear dream. My husband's friend died when his foot got caught. He hit the gas while going in reverse. He crashed in reverse. The dream deals with the future because I am standing on the porch looking out. I am fearing the future because I don't want my husband to die before me. This is my greatest fear and I have not conquered it yet.

A friend of mine has a fear dream often. Her first husband cheated on her many times. She is now remarried, and her second husband would never cheat in a million years, he just wouldn't, he is a great guy. Yet she dreams he cheats on her. It is a fear dream.

I don't believe God wants us to live with fear. I am not sure if fear dreams are God wanting us to deal with our fears or just a result of us harboring these fears. Either way, I believe the answer is to bring the fear to the Lord.

Chapter Seven

Questions to Ask

Asking questions helps us in the process of interpreting dreams. I want to go over some questions to ask.

What is Happening in my Life Right Now?

Most likely the dream you are having is dealing with what is going on in your life right now or what is about to go on. This could be a clue to the meaning of the dream.

I have also noticed that many times when an unsaved person tells me a memorable dream, that they have just had it is usually very obvious the dream has to do with their need to get right with God. Remember my troubling childhood dreams. They were dealing with the upheaval in my soul and my need for God and inner healing. So, looking at what is going on in your life at the time of the dream is a crucial question to ask yourself.

When I am writing a book, my dreams are a lot of time direction about my books.

I dreamt that there was a garage sale in a driveway between two houses. In the driveway was a long line of cars. I went to the two garage sales that were facing each other across the driveway. At the first garage sale everything cost fifty cents. I was thrilled because the prices were so good. At the second garage sale everything in it cost seven dollars. I thought, "That is just too expensive! I can't pay seven dollars!" But as I looked around at the seven-dollar stuff it was really good stuff.

In this dream God was speaking my language because I am the garage sale queen. I buy tons of stuff at garage sales. This dream was dealing with the book I was writing. The cars lined up in the driveway were chapters. The fifty-cent garage sale represented the stuff that did not cost me a lot emotionally, to write. The seven-dollar garage sale was things that were hard for me to write, it was an emotional cost. The Lord was encouraging me to write the things that were hard to write. I have tried to heed that dream. I have had to dig deep and write things that are hard for me to even talk about. There are even things written in my books that I had never told anyone.

While I am writing books, my dreams will commonly be about the books. That is what is going on in my life.

Also, I always pray as I am going to sleep. I have often noticed that what I prayed about as I went to sleep is the answer to what my dream means. So, when you are wondering what a dream means ask yourself:

What is the biggest issue in my life right now?

What have I been praying about?

What has God been dealing with me about?

These questions can help you interpret your dream or help you if you are interpreting a dream that is being told to you.

How is This Dream Like My Life?

This question helps me interpret my dreams more than any other thing. Just recently, I had a dream, and I woke up wondering why in the world I would dream such a thing. I dreamt about a friend of mine who had a horrible marriage. She married a man who was abusive and cheated on her, but his worst quality was he was annoying. He was horribly annoying. But that was years ago. She has since remarried a wonderful Christian man and is very happy.

I dreamt my friend got back with her old husband, and I was appalled. I thought doesn't she remember how annoying he is. Also, in the dream there was no reference to her new husband at all.

I was really perplexed why I would dream such a thing until a few days later, I had the same feelings that I had in the dream. I had been so tired of my job as a home health aide for many reasons. One was it takes up all my time, but I don't get paid for it. I would have to drive 45 minutes to work, work six hours drive forty five minutes home, be home for forty five minutes then drive back to work another twenty five minutes work two hours then twenty five minutes home, that would take me from around eight in the morning until seven at night, but for all that I would only get paid for an eight hour day and I would not get mileage because we only get mileage between houses and not from home. It was annoying! I had to have surgery which I usually hate because of the pain but I was actually looking forward to it just to get a break from my job. I did I got a six-week recovery period paid with saved up sick pay. I kept hoping the break would refresh me and I would no longer dread my job. I dreamt this dream my first week back to work. The dream was referring to my job! After six weeks away it was like going back to a bad marriage.

The breakthrough in determining the meaning of my dream was the feelings I was going through back at work were the feelings I was going through in the dream. It was like my life. The reason God gave me this dream is because changing jobs is a terrifying thought to me. He wants me to be ready when He brings me a new one. This dream could be called a perspective dream.

What is the Subject Matter or Focus of the Dream?

Try to pick out the main focus of the dream. Most often we dream about our own life, and we are the main focus of the dream. The dream is about us. Now what is the sub-focus? Try to simplify the message.

John Paul Jackson, who was a prophet and a dream expert, would have people name their dream. Then he would actually help people interpret their dream by drawing it out. In the center of the paper, he would put the focus of the dream. Which in most of our dreams we are the focus, the dream is about us. Then he would graph the sub focuses of the dream around the center. That would help him interpret the dream.

Let's try it. My daughter Lonna just called and told me her dream. Let's use hers.

Lonna dreamt that there was a sickness, and it could or could not be terminal. Because of it Lonna had to have something done at the doctor's office that would cost thousands, but she was not sure if her insurance company would pay for it. There was some confusion, but it turned out that, yes, her insurance company would pay for it. Then in the dream her dentist office canceled her appointment. The secretary bumped her appointment and it would be put off until later. Lonna noticed the dentist was really her eye doctor. Lonna felt like she should not get upset over all this that it was a test, and she should stay calm.

This dream has a lot of detail. So, first off let's name it and then let's pick out the main focus and the sub focuses,

Name: We will call it, The Canceled Dentist Appointment.

Focus: Lonna is the focus, the dream is about her

Sub focus: Sickness

Sub focus: Insurance fiasco

Sub focus: Canceled appointment, appointment put off

Sub focus: Lonna stays calm

Now let's talk about Lonna's life right now. One very interesting point is the day after the dream Lonna's dentist office really did call and canceled her appointment and she did not even realize she had an appointment. This dream happened during the coronavirus. Lonna had two jobs and she could go to neither because our governor shut down the whole state. Lonna was also having a struggle applying for unemployment.

This makes the dream easier to understand.

Focus: Lonna is dreaming about her life.

Sub focus: The sickness is the coronavirus; it affects everyone but for some it is terminal. It has affected Lonna because she can't go to work.

Sub focus: The insurance in her dream is about her Unemployment Compensation, she had trouble because the state was swamped with claims, and she was having trouble applying.

Sub focus: Lonna's life right now is put on hold.

Sub focus: The dentist who looks like her eye doctor is referring to two things. The dentist represents understanding, and eye doctor vision. Lonna does not know what will happen with her career, or her life at this point. She does not have understanding or vision what is going to happen so for now she needs to trust God with her future.

Sub Focus: Lonna has made a decision that this is a test, and she is trusting the Lord.

My favorite part of this whole dream is God's amazing sense of humor. Her real dentist called the next morning after the dream and canceled her appointment. As usual God is confirming the dream and I believe He is saying to her that everything is in His Hands!

This dream is meant to encourage Lonna and also is prophetic, it is letting her know everything will work out with her unemployment and that God is in control.

Why is This in the Dream?

A good question to ask yourself is, "why is this symbol in the dream?" Maybe in the dream you are driving a car, but it is not your car, why is it this vehicle? When a symbol in the dream stands out as different than your normal life, or unusual ask, "why?" For a long time in my dreams, I was in a school bus. "Why?" It was during a learning time in my life.

Remember my tornado dreams? They meant my husband was going to have a storm in his personality. I wrote about them earlier in the book. I had these dreams often and they would warn me a storm was coming, a meltdown, in Jim. I had one of these dreams almost five years ago. Jim had been sober for a long period and the storms had pretty much gotten better. This was several years after I wrote my book *The Impossible Marriage* and I was hoping there were going to be no more storms!

I dreamt that I was at my Aunt Delese and Uncle Don's house. A huge tornado came, and we got to the basement as the storm hit the house. The whole house shook as the storm roared with horrendous force, and it almost seemed as if it might be the end. But even though the house shook violently from the force of the storm, the house stood.

When I woke up, I didn't want to believe another storm was coming, it had been so many years I had thought they were over for good. But I wondered why this storm was at my aunt's house. Why not at my house? I prayed about it throughout the day and the answered popped into my head. It was the initials. A.D.D., Aunt

Delese and Uncle Don stood for ADD. Jim has severe A.D.D., Attention Deficit Disorder. The tornado had to do with ADD. I wondered what would happen.

Well, the storm came. Just like in the dream, it was one of the worst ones ever. Jim had a total meltdown. I could see it coming but I was so bogged down with work that I could not figure out why he was falling apart. I was trying to get him back on track, but his behavior was out of control

Jim is usually depressed. Depression Jim can deal with, but this was different. Jim was in a frenzy. It was like a mania. He wouldn't rest. He wasn't acting right. He was like a ball bouncing down a hill with no control. When I would go, to work, I would wonder what he was up to. One day I saw his car at a convenience store. I was in a hurry to get to my next patient, but I stopped and ran in the store. Jim was standing there with a fist full of money buying lottery tickets.

"Where did you get that money, "I demanded. We had no extra money. He wouldn't answer. I started smelling alcohol on his breath again. His mood and behavior became angry and explosive again. I tried taking his keys and credit cards in desperation. I tried to get him to stop and think. But he wouldn't stop, and he wouldn't think. It all came to a head when he was contacted by the police. They were going to charge him with a felony!

He was acting so crazy that I felt he needed to be

in a mental hospital. He was rocking and talking to himself and out of his head. It seemed like we were not going to make it this time. It seemed we came to the end, and that we wouldn't get through this one. Jim went down to the police station and confessed to what he had done. The police told them he would be charged with two felonies. They said to go home, and they would pick him up on Monday.

I finally found out what had spun Jim so far out of control. Jim had contacted his psychiatrist without my knowledge. He had put him on ADD medicine without my knowledge. I usually manage my husband's medicine. He had taken the whole bottle over a period of two or three weeks. That is what had caused his breakdown.

The police never came on Monday nor the next Monday. Jim decided to check into rehab to get back off alcohol while he was waiting to be arrested. He did not expect to get through rehab before they came, but he did. The weeks went by, and they did not come, but Jim was back on track. He completed rehab and stayed sober. Weeks, months, and several years went by. The police never arrested him. The storm rocked our household, but our house stood. This was all foretold in a dream!

What is the Setting?

What is the setting of your dream? The dream may deal with your family, your work, your church, your marriage, yourself, or a relationship, or many other things. The key will be in the setting. Different settings can mean different things. Remember the last dream I just talked about? The setting was my Aunt Delese and Uncle Don's house. The setting was ADD. The dream was about Jim's ADD.

Is the Dream Good or Bad?

It is funny that I have to answer this question, but I do. A lot of times a problem may show up in a dream and unless I ask this question I don't realize if the outcome is good or bad. Was the problem resolved in the dream? Many times, the answer is yes. Many times, I wake up and I don't know if it is resolved or not. This means it is time to pray!

I recently dreamed I was with my husband, and we were waiting for a train to start moving. We were in the last car. The train started, but we were not yet connected to the train. So, we had to wait some more. While we were waiting, I saw my mother off in the distance with my baby. I was worried about my baby, so I left Jim in the train to go get the baby. As I was getting my baby, the train started moving. I was frantic. I started chasing the train but couldn't catch it. I was so upset. The train curved around the track and came back by. As it passed, I saw the conductor, she was a beautiful woman. I begged her to please stop the train so I could get on with my husband. She did, and I ran to the car Jim was in and got in, with the baby.

When I woke up, I had no idea what the dream meant. I felt like I had been through such an emotional ordeal, but I asked myself was the dream good or bad? I had to really think and then answer, the dream was good! I did not miss the train. The conductor stopped the train for me, and I was able to get on.

This dream was so recent that even though I think I know the meaning; I am not sure. I believe the dream is me waiting for what God is about to do next. Which would be the train beginning to move. The baby is this book, which I had a lot of trouble getting started writing and finally I got going, but I almost missed the train. The good news is that although the train began to move, and I was late, I didn't miss it. I believe this book will be done on time, and I will be ready for what God is going to do next.

The whole point is I had to ask myself was the dream good or bad. It felt bad because I was so close to missing the train, but the outcome is good.

Chapter Eight

Symbols in Dreams

Dreams are written in God's symbolic language. Let's look at some of the main symbols to get an idea how to determine a dream's meaning.

Colors

Colors often hold the meaning to a dream. One time I had a dream that seemed like a bad dream, but the color was the key, it was not a bad dream.

I dreamt I was in a red van and a white van crashed into me and severely dented the car but didn't destroy it. "Oh no!" I cried, "What will I do now?"

I did not drive a red van. I had a blue Nissan Sentra. So, why did I dream I drove a red van?

My car was a huge issue. It had always been a huge issue with us, because we had, up to this point in our life, been a very low-income family. It had always been hard to keep a working car. But our car was especially crucial at this point, because our income at this time in our lives was a paper route that I was doing. I was delivering almost 500 papers a day. I was worried because my car was having problems. I had no money to fix it or get a new one. But I had a blue car, so why did I dream I drove a red van?

Well, I did not know what this dream meant until it happened. I was at a red light with my blue car when a huge semi-truck turned behind me. He got too close to me and started crushing my car. I beeped for him to stop but the left rear of my car had been smushed. The wheel wouldn't turn. At first, I thought my car was not drivable. But the truck driver who had hit me stopped and put the donut {spare tire] on my car. It was small enough that the tire would turn, and I could drive. It made me nervous but at least I could show up to work. After two weeks of driving on the donut the trucking company sent me fifteen hundred dollars to fix my car. I spent four hundred to get the car drivable, but I saved the rest of the money and didn't touch it. Soon after my engine went out on my car, and I used the money to buy a used station wagon. The accident turned out to be a blessing in disguise, which was what the dream was telling me. The clue was the car's colors.

Red, my vehicle was red I was covered with the blood of Jesus. He had my vehicle situation covered. White another good color. I was hit by a white car, but it was in His divine providence.

Here is another example of a dream that seemed bad, but the color was the clue. This dream also fore told a disaster that God had already knew and planned for. This dream came after we had bought an old fixer upper house from a man my husband knew, named Mr. Peters.

I dreamt we were in the new house and the water in the house overflowed and flooded the house. The only thing was the water was clear as crystal. "Oh no," I cried, "I will have to call Mr. Peters."

It seemed like a bad dream, but the clue was the clear water. Again, disaster soon happened. Not too long after we moved into the house the sewage backed up. When we called a repairman, he informed us the house had no drain field. After prayer I realized the answer was in the dream, it was to call Mr. Peters. I was scared to do it, but I did, I called him. Mr. Peters knew how to put in drain fields. He had my husband Jim do all the digging and he brought over the pipes and the gravel, and the problem was solved. The dream foretold the problem and the solution. The water in the dream was clear and clean. It meant God had the problem well at hand and to call Mr. Peters.

If a color stands out in a dream or is different than real life it is a clue to the meaning.

Numbers

The numbers in a dream can hold the key to the meaning. This dream I was able to interpret because of the numbers in it.

I dreamt of a friend of mine named Joe. The police pulled him over for speeding. The police officer said, "You were going 99 miles an hour, if you had gone one more mile faster, I would have arrested you."

This dream was actually about Joe. I was not in the dream. I just watched the dream about Joe. So that told me that Joe was the subject. Another clue you need to know is Joe's wife had left him and Joe was going through a very hard time. He was drinking and he was not serving the Lord like he had been. I knew it was because he was in so much emotional pain. Joe had lost everything.

The numbers 99 and 1 are from the Bible. Jesus said he would leave the ninety-nine sheep to find the one. This dream was answering something I was worried about. Was Joe still right with the Lord? The answer is yes. Joe was still in the ninety-nine, he was pushing it to the limit, but he was still in God's fold. Joe is remarried now and doing better.

In another dream I had the numbers were the key. *I dreamt I was riding an elevator up to the fifth floor, but I stopped and got off at the third floor instead.*

The dream was obvious to me because I had just fasted for three days. I had felt led to fast, something I hate to do. After three days I ate and, ate and ate. I realized from the dream that I was supposed to have fasted for five days not three.

Numbers are often the key to the dream, and many numbers have a meaning. I will put the meanings in the dictionary at the end of the book.

People

People in dreams can represent themselves, or most often they can be symbolic. Sometimes they might represent a certain trait that is dominant in them.

Once I dreamt of Mr.T. He picked me up in a car and kissed me.

Remember Mr. T was popular in the eighties? He was a big tough, black man who fought Rocky in one of the Rocky movies. No, I don't have a crush on Mr. T. But this was a very good dream. I have always been passive and let people walk all over me. This dream came when I started sticking up for myself. I was getting tough like Mr.T. Mr T was a part of my personality coming into balance.

Many times, the people in my dreams are all me, or all parts of me. Different parts of me that were in conflict with myself. This was a concept that was hard for me to grasp, but once I did, it helped me understand more dreams.

I had a dream I had a beautiful little girl. She was about two years old, and she had blonde hair and blue eyes. What made this little girl so adorable was she had such a feeling of sweetness about her. She was just precious. I spanked the little girl because I felt she was being naughty. When I spanked her, I thought that she couldn't feel it because she had a diaper on. So, I spanked her harder, and I still felt she couldn't feel it. So, I spanked her even harder. I pulled down her little diaper. I realized I had spanked her way too hard. She was black and blue. I felt terrible I had hurt her so terribly. I laid her in her crib. When I did, she laid in her crib and cried out to God because she was in so much pain. I listened to her desperate prayer to God.

I needed some help with this dream, I did not get it at first. The clue came when I went to bed the next night. Every night when I would lay in bed and before I would go to sleep, I would cry out to God in pain, emotional pain. It was a nightly ritual. My emotional pain was so severe I could not get to sleep at night without crying out to God. As I did, I realized that I was the precious little girl in the dream. The dream absolutely floored me because I realized through the dream that I was beating myself up! That was what was causing my emotional pain. I couldn't believe it at first, but it was true! I was causing my own pain!!!! I was being too hard on myself!!!

I also realized something else through the dream. If my spirit looked like that sweet little girl to the Father, then I was beautiful, because she had the sweetest spirit that radiated from her. This dream was an eye opener to me in several ways. It showed me something I did not know and that surprised me. It showed how I looked to God; I was beautiful inside. It also showed me to stop spanking myself!

I have had other dreams with more characters, and I was every character in the dream. One of the characters was a policeman. He was the authoritative side of me that was in conflict with another part of myself. There were four characters in that dream, and I was all four. I can't remember the dream well enough to retell it.

People in your dream can also represent the meaning of their name. Remember my first dream in the book. I was dreaming of the boy that drowned but he appeared as my grandson Franklin in the dream. This was because of the meaning in his name.

People in a dream may also represent their career. Such as the time I dreamt about my doctor.

I dreamt I was starving. All I had to eat was peanut butter. I had been told by a friend that peanut butter was not good for me. I thought I shouldn't eat it, but I could not help myself because I was so hungry. It was all I had to eat. In the dream I was voraciously eating the peanut butter. My doctor appeared in the dream. He picked up the jar of peanut butter and read the label. "This is good for you," he declared, "It has vitamins in it."

The doctor represented wisdom, or even indirectly

the Lord. To understand this dream, you would have to know what I was going through at the time of the dream.

I had been going through several years of a demonic attack. When I had prayer at church it only got worse. It did get worse and worse. Finally, I felt led to read a book by a man who called himself an exorcist. The book was radical, that was for sure. So was the man. I went to him for help. Some people from my church did not want me to go. They warned me not to see him, that he was strange. That is when I had this dream.

I was starving because I had no help for my problem. I had been told not to eat the peanut butter because it was not good for me. That was the advice from the well-meaning people at my church. I was torn at what to do, because I was so hungry that I needed the peanut butter. I was confused if I was doing the right thing going to the exorcist, {who was a wonderful Christian man}. The dream was showing me, that I needed the help the man was giving me and that it was good. The doctor {the expert, wisdom or the Lord} was giving me permission to continue getting help. Which I did, and I stopped worrying that I was doing the wrong thing.

{The whole story is in my book, *Satan Has No Power Over You*}

Animals

Animals in dreams can mean many different things also. They can represent a dominant trait. Such as an owl may stand for wisdom, or a beaver may be industrious, or an otter may stand for playfulness. They can stand for other things also.

My son, Jamie went through some years with turbulent emotions. And he had plenty of reasons to be frustrated, growing up in an alcoholic home was hard. He had severe learning disabilities. And his big frustration was, he was the only boy in a household of four girls. {He was soooo tired of girls} What made things worse was he had to share a bedroom with his two little sisters until he was fourteen years old. He was frequently frustrated. When he was about eight years old, the Lord led me to take the kids and stay in a motel for four months. {It was a cheap motel.} I needed to pray and fast and work on my parenting skills. It was an intense time; the Lord allowed no television and there was plenty of time to work on the kid's behavior. {I wrote more about this in my book, *The Impossible Marriage*.} After we had been there for a while Jamie told me his dream.

"Mom, I dreamt I married a little girl, and we went to the zoo and all the animals were quiet,"

This was a good dream. Jamie marrying a little girl meant balance in his personality. The zoo with the quiet animals were his emotions. They had settled down. So, animals in Jamie's dreams stood for emotions.

If an animal is chasing you in your dream, your emotions may be out of control, or you may not be in touch with your emotions. Maybe something is making you very angry, and you can't express it.

Sometimes an animal in your dreams may stand for a person. I had a series of dreams about our dog Sam. I realized that Sam stood for my husband Jim. I wondered why at first, but it soon became obvious Jim and Sam were inseparable. If Jim were a dog, he would look like Sam. So, Sam stood for Jim.

Another time an animal stood for a person. I had a horrible experience on my job as a home health aide. I was sent to a new man's house. When I got there, it was a nightmare. The place stunk to high heavens. I soon found out why. The man who was partially paralyzed was sitting in a chair stark naked, covered in poop. He had smeared it all over himself. {He never wore clothes he stayed stark naked every time I was there.} He was waiting for me to clean him up.

The place was a house of horrors. It was a tiny apartment, but every nook and cranny were stocked with foul, foul porn movies and magazines. It was so awful there that after my shift I went home and cried. I was hoping I would never have to go back. Then they put him on my schedule several days a week. I was horrified. I decided to just do the best I could. I started putting a towel over him when I got there. I cleaned his house the best I could. I cleaned him the best I could. I did the best I could. I ignored the filthy porn, the best I could.

Soon a skunk started showing up in my dreams. I thought the Lord had forgotten all about being Lord of my life and handling my life. I thought He had let the devil take over. But I learned through my dreams, that the Lord was pleased with my efforts to care for this man. The man I was caring for was the skunk, showing up in my dreams. I am glad I passed that test quickly. Soon I was assigned somewhere else.

One time, I had a very vivid dream that I was looking out the window and I saw a Tiger. I was so shocked that a tiger was running loose right outside. Then I saw a bear, it was foreign looking not the kind we have in Michigan. My emotions in the dream were absolute shock and I realized it was not safe to be outside, that there were wild animals prowling around. I woke up and still felt shocked. I wondered what in the world could it mean. When I prayed, I felt the Lord say it was about terrorists. That there are terrorists present in our country. The dream was God revealing a danger that has come to our country.

I want to talk about one more animal that showed up in my dreams. For years, I dreamed about a parrot. I am not a person that would ever want to have a pet. I am not comfortable around animals. Although I grew to love our dog Sam, it took years, but I was never exactly comfortable around him. My husband and children are animal people. So here comes my husband home with a parrot. He named him Julio because he was some kind of South American parrot.

Julio hated me. He was jealous of me because he was so attached to Jim. Most of the time he was in his cage, but if he got out, which he sometimes did, he would attack me. He would fly into my face and bite me. I actually had cuts on my face from his sharp beak. I got so scared that if I saw him out of his cage I would fall to the floor and hide my face. Then he would land on the back of my head and start ripping out my hair with his beak. It got to the point that I told my husband it was me or Julio. So, Julio went.

I had nightmares of Julio chasing me for years after that. Julio became a symbol of a small thing that scared me. A lot of small things scare me a lot, so it seemed I was always dreaming of Julio chasing me.

Babies

Babies in a dream are the new thing God is doing in your life. When I started writing my first book, *The Impossible Marriage,* I kept dreaming about a baby. The book was the baby.

I dreamt my daughter left her baby boy in the car. I was so upset and chewed her out. "You can't just go away and leave your baby unattended!" I told her.

The dream was a message to me. I was my daughter, and I was me. I had put the book down, and I hadn't worked on it for two weeks. I had left the baby unattended. I knew I had to get back to writing again.

I frequently dream of babies. It is not too hard to figure out what is new in my life, and what the dream is about.

Another time God had been speaking to me to write a letter to a man I knew. I tried and tried to write the letter, but I wasn't sure what the Lord wanted me to say. So, I gave up.

I dreamt I had a miscarriage. I was very sad.

When I woke up, I knew I had missed out on something God wanted to birth in my life and it had to do with the letter that I couldn't get written.

Houses or Buildings

Houses can mean many different things in a dream. I often dream of past houses I have lived in. Such as the house my husband and I bought before we got married. Our marriage started there. So, dreaming of this house has to do with our marriage, or that time period.

Dreaming of a house can also refer to your soul or your personality. Both my twin sister and I had the same dream. I had it many times. *I dreamt I found new rooms I had never knew were there in my house. One of the rooms was big billiard room. I would be amazed when I discovered these rooms in my house because I never knew they were there.*

Carol, my twin sister, is the one who discovered what our hidden billiard room dreams meant. About five or six years ago, she felt compelled to find out something about our birth father whom we knew nothing about. Her compulsion to find him came the same week he died. She found his obituary and discovered we had many brothers and sisters and a family we never knew. Our birth father that we never knew played billiards as well as the rest of the family all play billiards. It was a hidden part of us we never knew was there.

Sometimes the floor of the house I am in stands for something. A higher floor may mean my spirit and a lower floor may be my natural self.

I dreamt of a bank, the ground floor had crowded offices cheap paneling and was chaotic looking, but the next floor was beautiful. It had marble floors and was spacious and perfect looking.

I was dreaming of my spiritual walk with the Lord which was very beautiful and high quality. But the ground floor was my life as I live on earth. I was poor and unsuccessful. The dream was dealing with my inability to carry my rich spiritual life into my natural life. It was a lesson God was teaching me. I needed to bring the higher realm into reality with the earthly realm.

Dreaming of an attic can represent a part of you that is not seen or stored away.

Someone told me of a dream they had that something was falling out of the attic. It was red and she thought it was fire. She stopped to look at it and picked it up and realized it was lasagna. Then she realized that someone was living in the attic and the lasagna was dropping down from the attic.

The dream was fascinating. She was the one living in the attic. Her mother was Italian, and her father was a black man. She had rejected the Italian part of her personality and that part of her was living in the attic. God wanted her to accept the other side of her heritage. What was even more fascinating was the next day she went to work, and they had a surprise dinner for the employees. It was lasagna and she said it was sooo delicious. God was confirming her dream and showing her how delicious that part of her was.

Dreaming of a house can even mean your physical body. For a period of time, I kept having the same dream over and over. I didn't like the dream.

I would dream I was looking at the foundations of my house and I would find the house was rotting. I would realize that it could not be repaired, and I would think, "Oh no, where will I live?"

This dream kept repeating itself. I found out the

dream was my body, I had cancer. I had uterine cancer and they found it in time. I had a total hysterectomy and the dream never returned.

Houses stand for many things. I have even had houses stand for days of my lives.

I was driving through neighborhoods seeing house after house lined up together, for miles and miles and miles. The houses started off nice and then the neighborhood got shabbier.

The dream was exactly what was happening in my life. Day after day of going to work and my job was getting less and less enjoyable.

Vehicles

Vehicles are one of the most common symbols in my dreams. When I dream that I am driving in a car, I am dreaming about my life. Which car am I driving in? What kind of car? What color is the car? Is this a car you have owned? There are so many different kinds of vehicles. What are you driving in and why?

I have dreamt this, or something very similar, many times.

I am driving along in a car, then I am on a bicycle, pretty soon I am trudging along on foot.

This dream is showing how the thing I am going through in my life at the time is taking more and more effort and getting more difficult.

I frequently dream, *I am driving in my car, and I try*

to step on the brakes and the car will not stop all the way.

This is just showing my inability to stop something in my life I want stopped or needs to be stopped.

I dreamt I was riding on a school bus. The driver was a man that had been burned in an airplane crash. His face was scarred. The bus turned over and my kids and I escaped out of the back-emergency exit.

The school bus represents a time of learning. The driver represents suffering. I am learning through suffering. The bus turning over, and the escape was what we were going through at the time. For a short time at the Lord's direction my children and I left my husband, and our life was disrupted. You can see this vehicle represented a time of learning in my life.

I dreamt I was riding a train. It was a strange way to ride a train, you sat on the top of it like a horse. I was trying to hang on, but I kept sliding off. The people around me kept pulling me back up but I kept slipping and I was barely hanging on.

The dream was about me and about church. The train stood for training. We had a new pastor that I just could not follow his teaching. I really liked him a lot, he was a wonderful man. But I was so bored at church I kept thinking of excuses not to go. I thought of changing churches. What kept me hanging on was how much I cared for the people at my church. The problem resolved when the pastor left and was replaced with just the right man.

One vehicle dream I had was a warning to me. In real life had recently gone to the bank to apply for a second mortgage because I was having trouble making ends meet. *I dreamt I was in a large heavy black truck and the driver was the loan officer at the bank. We drove from the lower peninsula of my home state of Michigan to the upper peninsula. Once we crossed over to the upper peninsula the truck broke down. I said, "Uh-oh, how will we get back." Then I woke up.*

I realized the dream was a warning not to get the loan. The lower peninsula stood for my mortgage and the upper peninsula stood for a second mortgage. The big black truck stood for debt. I knew the Lord was warning me that I would get over my head with too much debt and I did not go through with the loan. I managed to catch up with the Lords help and no loan.

The same symbol reappeared in another dream several years later. *I dreamt a large black truck crashed into my garage and hit the house hard enough to crack the picture window.* At first, I did not know what the dream meant. It had been many years since the first black truck dream, and I had forgotten the symbol. What helped me interpret the dream was what was happening at the time of the dream. I had checked my credit report and my credit had dropped drastically from over 800 to the 600's. I found out it was because I had helped someone by cosigning for a car and they had missed a payment. It upset me because I had some medical debts, I was having trouble getting paid and then this. The dream was about debt again. The reason that it hit the house and broke the picture window was because it affected my peace. My outlook became affected. The answer was for me to talk to the person who I co-signed for, which I did, and get back into peace.

Biblical Symbols

The Bible has a lot of symbolism to look for, the parables are a great place to start.

Fields- the world

Seed- the word of God

Birds- the enemy to steal the word

Fish- are souls

Thorns- the cares of life

Soil-the heart

The Good Shepherd-Jesus

Wolves-false prophets

Yeast of the Pharisees- their religious, self-righteous teaching

Or how about the symbols from the Pharaoh's dream?
Seven fat cows- seven years of plenty

Seven skinny cows- seven years of famine

But there are symbols throughout the Bible

Rainbows-covenant

Lamb- Jesus

Snake-sin

Jesus

Jesus rarely appears to me in my dreams as Himself. He usually appears as my husband Jim. But not every time that I dream of Jim, will he stand for Jesus. When Jim stands for Jesus in a dream, I have noticed that He usually comes in response to my screaming for help, but He doesn't hurry. He moves steadily and deliberately but He does not run.

I dreamt I was standing in the backyard and looking into the woods. I could see all kinds of wildlife in the woods, and they scared me but fascinated me. Suddenly a wolf ran out of the woods and attacked me. He took my head in his mouth. In the dream I screamed for Jim, Jim immediately pulled up in a blue pick-up truck. He got out and walked over to me and gave me aid. Then the scene changed, and I saw a doctor at the hospital, he said, "Summer will survive;

she needs to drink vinegar and water."

The dream was dealing with a generational curse that attacked my health. Being in the backyard represents the past and looking deep into the woods and seeing the wild animals represented the generational curses. I called for Jim because Jim is not afraid of animals and that is what I would have done had something like that really happened to me. In the dream the Lord was giving me literal instructions to drink vinegar and water. I know because the next day my daughter Lonna said to me, "Mom, I feel you need to start drinking vinegar and water." The Lord confirmed the dream.

But let's deal with why the Lord did not appear as Himself. I believe it was because the dream had a specific message and had He appeared as Himself I would have been so excited about seeing Him, even in a dream, that I would not have heard His message.

I have to tell you this happened to me once. I was in bed and the Lord was giving me some specific instructions. He was speaking to Me very clearly which was kind of unusual. I got up and I saw Him standing at the end of the hall. What a thrill it was! It was the only time I have ever got a really good look at Him in that way. I had lots of pictures of Jesus hanging in my room and I had always been curious what He really looked like. I had always wanted to see Him!

I started screaming and yelling to everyone in the

house, particularly my mom and dad that Jesus was in the hall. I kept running back and forth and checking if He was still there. I was so excited that if He was planning on saying something to me, I missed it in my excitement.

{If you wanted to know what He looked like, He looked very much like Salman's Christ.}

I believe that is why Jesus does not appear as Himself in our dreams. So as not to distract from the message. My daughter had this experience also.

She dreamt she was talking to a man who had a name tag that said Phillip. His countenance was so beautiful she asked Him if He were an angel, and He said, "No."

Then she asked, "Are You the Lord?"

He said, "Yes."

"Well why does your name tag say Phillip?" she asked Him.

The Lord replied, "Because you need to fill up."

I believe the Lord did not want to distract her from the message He was bringing. That message was her spiritual oil was getting low.

I have only had one dream in my life where the Lord appeared as Himself. And in that dream, I did not get to look directly into His face. Still that dream had a huge impact on me. It is thrilling to be in the Lord's presence.

The dream started with me underwater. Jesus came up and pulled me out of the water. He put His one arm around me, and we walked together while with the other hand He held a bible and read to me.

I had this dream shortly after I came to the Lord and was baptized. I woke up so in love with Jesus, and that was the point. It was just about Him showing me He loved me. I was thrilled and that was okay. But I get so ga ga over Jesus that He doesn't appear as Himself in my dreams.

Angels

Angels are frequently in dreams, but they don't look like angels. It took me awhile to recognize them in my dreams. Like in one dream I was in a hotel. I was asking the hotel clerk a question. I knew she was an angel by the way she acted. She had a knowing look on her face.

Another time when God had directed me to go from Florida to Michigan for a time of prayer and fasting, I kept dreaming of park rangers. *I dreamt I drove up a big snowy mountain in a big white pickup truck with an emblem and the park rangers were escorting me. They did not talk much they were just there to help.* I went surrounded by angels.

The Holy Spirit

The Holy Spirit will often be in your dreams because He is your constant companion. Remember Jesus called Him the Helper. So, the Helper in your dreams may be Him. He is usually someone near you, but you never see His face. His name is also Comforter so He may appear in your dreams as a Comforter. He is very humble and frequently He is someone near you who is faceless. You will never quite get a look at His face. Or He may even appear as someone who brings you comfort like a favorite dog who was a constant companion, or someone you feel close to.

Falling

I have had many falling dreams in my life. I also have a terrible fear of heights. Falling in my childhood dreams were a result of the emotional torment I was in and how easily my world could come crashing in around me. I was emotionally unbalanced and unsecure, and I was being left with people I shouldn't have been. The falling was the result of the unstable situation I was in.

I have also had falling dreams in my adult life also. They can mean a loss of income, like a job loss or like the last falling dream I had was a huge emotional crash.

I dreamt I was on a huge rollercoaster. It went up very high. I was up way high into the sky, and I realized I was going to fall. I felt that familiar horror as I began to fall, but I fell into the ocean and a speed boat rescued me. I woke up heart pounding.

I did not know what the dream meant until a few days later when I experienced such a huge emotional letdown. The feeling felt so similar to the falling in the dream, that I realized this was the dream. It had to do with my first book, *The Impossible Marriage.* It had been published for several months. I had no idea how many copies it had sold but I knew a royalty check was coming in February. I had such high hopes. After all God had told me to write the book. I hoped He was going to make it successful. I was even hoping it may supplement my income. But my hi-hopes were dashed. When I got my royalty check it was only sixty-seven dollars. I was crushed. And that was the biggest royalty check I received.

The feeling I had was just like I was falling. I had a sick feeling in my stomach for days. I was really let down. I had to let go of all my expectations and just write books out of obedience to God. That is what I have done. I have been writing books now for nine years straight, which takes a lot of my time. I write out of obedience to God. Some of my books have not sold at all. They are God's to do with what He wants.

Falling in dreams has to do with some kind of let down or loss of support.

Crashes

Crashes in dreams can indicate a disaster. My daughter had a dream of an airplane crash. This dream came during her first marriage. She had a hard time in her first marriage. She had caught her husband cheating several times and even filed for divorce. Each time she did her husband would beg forgiveness and then become very charming for a time. She would always cave into him and each time she would drop the divorce. Then the whole situation would begin again. She was trapped in a hopeless situation. Then she had this dream.

Joy dreamed she was in an airplane with her husband, and he was flying it. The plane crashed, it snapped in half and was beyond repair. The plane landed in a cavern, like a hollowed-out mountain and she was trapped inside. She was also trapped in the wreckage and could not get out. She wanted to save her husband but realized she could not. She very slowly made her way out of the wreckage and slowly climbed up the cavern walls to escape.

The Lord spoke to Joy about the dream. He told her that her marriage was over, but it would take time to get out of it. It did, it took two years. Even though her situation was hopeless the dream encouraged her, gave her clarity and perspective. Because the pain of the marriage was so devastating, knowing God had a plan brought her hope.

Crashes in dreams have to do with something being destroyed. Remember my dream of my parents' divorce? That was also symbolized by a crash. Their marriage was symbolized by a car and a train crashed right through the middle of it, throwing each of them in a different direction and wounding my mother. Crashes are usually not good.

Chasing Dreams

Someone or something chasing you is very

common. There can be several reasons you are being chased in a dream.

Something needs your attention. You may be chased by the police in your dream. The police may represent your conscience, you are doing something wrong, and you know it.

Or you may have a burglar sneaking in the back door, and you just can't escape him. The thief may be a demonic force or a generational curse from your past. The answer is to find out how this is getting in and get rid of it through prayer.

Chasing dreams mean that there is something you need to deal with. Are you ignoring your own emotions? I have even heard of men being chased by a woman in their dreams when they are ignoring their softer side.

A dream of charging animals could be out of control emotions, or you are out of touch with your emotions, and they are trying to get your attention.

My husband Jim recently told me of a vivid nightmare he had the last time he was in rehab, which was just a couple of months ago. This was big, because according to Jim he rarely dreams.

Jim dreamt he was the group of people from his rehab and they were on their way to a twelve-step meeting. Jim got separated from the group when a man pulled up in a car to attack him. At first, the man seemed friendly but then he made a move that frightened Jim.

From that point in the dream, he was being chased. At one point he tried to fight with an antenna he was using like a sword. He kept running and the dream ended with a man coming up behind him and grabbing him, he woke up in terror.

The situation of this dream is about his rehab. He was in rehab at the time he dreamt it. He was with his rehab group in the dream, and he was on his way to a twelve-step meeting. The situation is definitely about his attempt to beat addiction.

The fact that he got separated from his group heading to a meeting is not good. He is being waylaid on his route to recovery. I find it interesting that Jim fought off his attacker with an antenna. In our day, televisions always had an antenna, and you even had to move it around to get a picture.

Jim has voices in his head that torment him. He combats it by keeping the television going. {I hate television} He turns it on the first thing when he wakes up in the morning and it is the last thing to go off at night and sometimes, I have to get up and turn it off. He keeps those voices in his head quiet by watching television. It anesthetizes him. This dream helped me in a way because I constantly complain about the television. It helped me to realize why he is watching it. Obviously from the dream it is only a temporary fix.

Finally, he is attacked from behind and wakes up.

This is pretty much the same meaning as the wake-up dream I had when he was being attacked. His last battle, the one with addiction is a battle with past abuse he needs healing from.

I keep this situation in constant prayer because Jim is not able to talk about his past. That is very rare.

Jim is being chased in his dream because his past needs to be dealt with and is causing his addiction problems.

If you are being chased in your dreams there is something you need to deal with, and like Jim you may need help.

Chapter Nine

Different Ways to Interpret a Dream

The interpretation of a dream can come differently each time. Here are some different ways.

1.It's obvious

Sometimes it is just obvious what the meaning of a dream is. Like a dream I had recently.

I dreamt I was standing on the edge of the water with my grandson. A man who was a helper throughout the dream was showing us how to catch fish. He was using a very simple pole with no rod and no reel, just a pole, a line and a hook. I was just telling him I never catch much when I pulled in a huge beautiful red fish. I laid it down and began fishing some more, when I looked over at my fish, he had turned white. The next fish I caught actually jumped up before my hook hit the water and hooked himself, again I was amazed. Then my grandson caught a black and purple fish. The man who was the helper said, "you can't keep those, that is a Marlin." So, he threw it back in. Then things got crazier, the fish started crawling out of the water on their own! I couldn't believe it.

As I was fishing, I realized this pool of water was in a house. The water level had risen up so high that it had created this unique fishing experience. I realized the water would soon recede and the fishing would be over.

When I woke up the dream was obvious to me. Fishing was a metaphor Jesus used with His disciples about making them fishers of men. I was catching souls which amazed me. I have never been a good soul winner before. Our helper was either the Holy Spirit or an angel, probably the Holy Spirit. My fish was red when I caught him then turned white was also obvious, "though your sins be as scarlet they shall be as white as snow." {Isaiah}

The fish my grandson caught, that had to be thrown back was witchcraft. It was black and purple and a Marlin which sounds a lot like Merlin. And the pool coming up from the flood was the floods of adversity which temporarily made people seek the Lord, which my guess is the corona virus. The waters would soon recede and the opportunity for fishing in this pool would pass.

2. Pray and Look Up Symbols

Many times, I receive a dream and I have no idea what it means. I will pray and ask God. I will dig out all my dream symbol guides, and I will ask myself questions.

I dreamt I was walking down a city block. As I was passing each house there would be a tree in the front yard of each house. Each tree was unique and had different things hanging on them. I was amazed at the beauty of the trees. Some were so beautiful they had crystals hanging in them, one even had angels in the tree.

I could not figure out what this dream meant until I started digging through dream symbol manuals. When I looked up street, and a city street with blocks and curbs, meant a rigid lifestyle. I knew I was dreaming about work. It put it all together for me. The trees were the people I met, and many older people would tell me their life stories and their family histories. Those were the beautiful trees I was seeing.

Another time I had a dream, and I had no clue what it meant.

I dreamt I was standing outside a fence it may have been near a school watching people playing different sports. I was watching and watching but the fence was between me and the playing field.

I would have never figured this one out without a dream dictionary. I looked up the symbol of the games, and it said that they represented the game of life. Well, this one fits me to a T. I have never been in on the game of life. I have never been successful. I have only had a few times had a savings account with a little money in it. The only reason we have a house was a complete miracle of God! In the game of life, I only seemed to be a watcher.

So, when I figured out the meaning, I wondered why I dreamt it, what did it mean to me? So, I began to pray. Through prayer the Lord showed me why I dreamt it. I was not familiar with business kind of stuff, but this is what I realized. We had recently bought our house and our mortgage rate was 8 percent. The rates at the time of the dream had dropped very low. By the time I realized the dream was telling me to watch the interest rates, {something I knew nothing about} they had gone back up. The good news is from that time on I did watch the interest rates. And when they went low again, I refinanced my house, and my payments went down considerably. God was getting me in on the game of life and making me a winner, through this dream. To interpret this dream, it took the dream dictionary, but it also took prayer for the answer.

3. God Plainly Tells You

My favorite way to interpret a dream is when God just plainly tells me what it means.

I dreamt of a town named Clio, my husband and I had lived in many years ago after we had only been married a few years. I dreamt I was going through the town and there were beautiful monuments there. {In real life there were no beautiful monuments} I was going through the town and stopping at these beautiful things that were throughout the town. One was a beautiful colored fountain. The others were also very beautiful and every time I got near to one of them, I would get the most wonderful feeling imaginable. I wanted to move there to be near the monuments.

When I woke up and started praying about the dream the Lord just plainly spoke to me. He said, "When you lived in Clio that was the hardest time of your life. You went through many trials. Now those things you went through have become monuments of blessing to yourself and others. I have made beauty from your trials."

Many of those trials we went through there I wrote about in my first book, *The Impossible Marriage.*

I was glad God plainly told me the dreams meaning I would not have known otherwise but it was a wonderful dream and a wonderful meaning.

4. Circumstances

The circumstances you're in will often interpret a dream for you.

My daughter dreamed she was at a beautiful banquet eating beautiful food. She just wished her husband could be there too.

My daughter and sister and I were scheduled to go to a Christian conference that weekend. She was dreaming of the rich teaching we were going to enjoy and did. And yes, her husband was not able to go. The dream was obvious because of the circumstances.

5. You Don't Know

There are dreams that I have never figured out, many, many, many. My best advice is to pray about it and leave it on the shelf for now. You can always pray about a dream, especially one that troubles you. If a dream really troubles me, I try to go back in the dream and just picture Jesus there. I ask Him to fix things.

6. Talk it Over with a Prayer Partner

Sometimes just talking it over with a prayer partner can help bring the meaning to light. Two of my prayer partners are my two beautiful daughters, Joy and Lonna, many times they can tell me what my dream means when I can't figure it out myself.

Chapter Ten

Confirmation of Dreams

God really wants to communicate with you through your dreams and He will very often confirm your dream the next day, or soon after. If you are sensitive, you will realize it happens very often.

Remember my dream in chapter one? I dreamt of the giant eagle, and I was wrestling with him. I was eye to eye with his huge golden eye. That next morning as I was pulling out of the driveway, I saw the wooden statue my husband had put there of an eagle, it had a golden eye. I had never noticed it before. It sent chills down my spine. As I looked at it the emotions from the dream came rushing back to me. It kept the dream fresh in my mind. The Lord wanted me to get the message in my dream and

He brought confirmation.

Also, the time I woke up held a message for me also. I woke up at 5:58. It stood for Isaiah 55:8 **For My thoughts are not Your thoughts, nor are your ways my ways says the Lord.**

I wanted God to save the boy but that was not His will or His way. God was letting me know through the time on the clock that His ways are not my ways but His are the best. It was more comfort and confirmation from the Lord that the boy who had drowned was in His hands.

One day I knew I had a dream because I had a feeling when I woke up, a feeling like I had a dream. I wanted to remember it, but I could not. The feeling persisted throughout the day and yet I could not remember it. During work I had to grocery shop for a patient and when I was grocery shopping and saw the food the whole dream came back, because the dream was about food. This is very common, often a symbol from the dream will appear in my life the next day, and all the emotions from the dream come flooding back to me. Suddenly I remembered the whole dream, the food jogged my memory.

Remember the dream we talked about earlier, the girl who dreamed of lasagna and the next day at work was a surprise luncheon of lasagna and it was soooo good! This was a continuation of the message from the dream and confirmation. God does this so often.

Remember my dream of the big black dogs in chapter two. In the dream my dad had come in and pointed out I had an infection. The next day he really did come in and talk to me about fear. His talk interpreted the dream for me. But the next day at church the sermon was everything dad had said to me. God confirmed to me over and over His message. It is amazing to me how much trouble God goes through to speak to each of us. He really hits the message home.

I was watching a sermon by Troy Brewer the other day on YouTube. He told about his dream. *He dreamt he floated up to the ceiling and banged his head. The knock on his head actually woke him up.*

He said he got up, went into his kitchen to make some coffee and dropped something. He bent down to pick it up and banged his head on the table! That was a confirmation of his dream. When he stood up rubbing his head the Lord spoke to him, "You are going to hit some ceilings you need to break through."

It blows my mind how God comes up with this stuff. He is always confirming things in miraculous and ingenious ways. It makes me ask myself, "How does He do all this stuff?" The answer is because He is so amazing, He is God!

Chapter Eleven

We Are Complex Beings

Beloved, now we are children of God and it has not yet been revealed what we shall be, but we know that when he is revealed, we shall be like him, for we shall see him as He is 1 John 3:2,

We are created in God's image, and we are very complex beings. I wrote about this in my book, *Created in His Image.* There is no other being quite like us because we were created to be God's children. Right now, we look nothing like what we will become, and right now we look nothing like Adam did in the garden. When we fell, we fell a long way. Our souls are very complex, and we are more than we realize. There is a world inside of each of us that no one knows except for God, Himself. We are even a mystery to ourselves, at least I know I was to myself.

I did not know myself. I could not understand the people around me, I felt like a little girl in a grown-up body, and every day was a challenge. Happy, confident people just amazed me, and I didn't know how to be like them. I was not capable of living like that. We have to understand that we are eternal beings, and our past is still living and sometimes those pasts have to be dealt with, and they show up in our dreams. Like my dream, my nightmare, of the door in the back of the closet. Part of my soul was locked in torment.

I still did not understand about my other childhood nightmare, the lady with the safari suit. The one about the lady in the safari suit that would take my mother and sister and me and cut us up into little pieces. What was that about and who was she?

A few years ago, I told my prayer partner Rhonda about the dream and the lady in the safari suit, and she prayed and immediately she said, "She's your grandma."

"No," I objected, "My grandma was the most important person in the world to me." But I looked. I looked into the dream, and I looked, and it was my grandma. She was a tall lady with red curly hair. She was a little younger than I remember grandma, but she was my grandma, and she was wearing a safari suit and hat. {it was actually a dress, grandma was born 1898, she did not wear pants}. Why was my grandma the lady in the safari suit? I didn't get it.

I do now and I will try to explain it. God had told me in my thirties to ask my mother about my birth. I knew nothing. All I knew was my birth father's name, I did not know what my mother had been through, and I did not realize how much it affected me.

It all started at church one day. I was standing in a big line for prayer. Rodney Howard Browne was visiting our church and he and our pastor were praying for thousands of people. The line probably went for a mile. They lined us up in the foyer that encircled the five thousand seat auditorium and into the lobby and anywhere they could fit people.

They went through the prayer line quickly and as they prayed the power of God would hit each person, and they would fall on the floor. It is called being slain in the spirit.

They had a group of ushers called catchers that would stand behind each person and lay them on the floor if they fell. There were about twenty catchers who would line up to catch someone and then run forward and stand behind someone else and on and on. It was quite a job because our pastor and Rodney would come through fast touching each one.

I was in that line. As they came through and prayed for me, I fell. The person ahead of me had fallen and landed kind of towards me and the person after me had fallen and fell faster and beat me to the floor. When I fell the usher behind me had nowhere to put me. I sat crumpled up between the two people on either side of me.

A horrible feeling came over me and I sat there and cried because there was no place for me. I felt so rejected I cried. I said, "God, you did not even save a piece of the floor for me."

I did not realize that God had this happen for a reason. He was about to deal with the person who was emotionally cut into pieces on the inside of me.

God spoke to me and said, "Summer you have felt like this your whole life. You have felt like there is no place for you."

That was so true.

Then God added, "I want you to ask your mother about your birth."

That is when I found out about all my mother went through and how her parents rejected her during our birth. After I learned this, while I was praying, I actually had a memory of being born. The memory was the feeling of not wanting to be born and rejecting my life. I was fighting not to be born.

God also showed me I was in a small way reliving my birth every morning when I woke up, my first thought of the day would be I don't want to wake up. I did not feel like I belonged here. I felt I had no right to be here. God spoke to me and told me, "This is my world and I put you here, you have every right to be here."

So, what does all this have to do with the lady in the safari suit? The rejection from my grandmother affected me in the womb and it cut me to pieces. Of course, I had no ought against her because I loved my grandma dearly. She was a wonderful grandmother, and I had no memory of rejection from her, except in my dreams, but it was something that needed to be dealt with. It has to do with our human soul and the past still exists, but with God, especially the work of the Holy Spirit, and the sacrifice of Jesus, the past can be redeemed.

Satan tries to destroy and shatter our souls and many times he is successful even while we are still in the womb. Many children are literally destroyed in the womb. God loves us so dearly that He will gently and lovingly restore and repair us, no matter what it costs Him or how long it takes.

Even though God has been seemingly healing our past for years Carol, my twin and I recently had a conversation. We were talking about my dreams of the lady in the safari suit. I was thinking about it again because I was working on this book. We had both received so much healing from the past but still I had some concerns.

"I still feel cut out of the family somehow." I told my sister and she agreed.

"It seems like we fell through the cracks. Like we were cut off from the family line. No one else in our family seems to have our struggles."

Our grandparents were very prosperous people, so were our parents, at least compared to us.

Thankfully, our children seemed to have become successful people, we felt like whatever it was, we did not pass on what was passed on to us. Even my mom's second family, the children she had after she and my dad divorced, were doing very well.

But Carol and I, our whole life seemed under a constant struggle, not just financially but also emotionally. We constantly fight depression. We call each other for comfort because we both experience the same thing.

We wondered if there was still more to our broken past we needed to come out of. We prayed about it together. We came before the courtroom of heaven and asked God the righteous judge to reverse any curse against us that may have come from our grandmother rejecting our arrival on earth. I didn't feel any different after the prayer but I still felt we were on to something.

A couple of weeks later Carol and I went to a Christian Conference. This was very rare. We left our husbands at home and went. The speaker was one of our favorites and when we found out he was coming to Michigan we were determined to go, and we did.

The speaker is not one who has altar calls or prays

personally for people, it is just not the way he does things. But he did. He called up people who were battling depression. I actually felt something push me up to the front. Carol was right behind me. It was one of those divine appointments. I felt something change. That was only a month ago, so we are still going through changes. But something is different.

We are truly complex, and we are fearfully and wonderfully made in His image. So, God solved another of my nightmares, the one with the woman in the safari suit. It had to do with rejection from before we were born. And just recently one last layer of that rejection was removed.

Remember my last nightmare, the dream of playing a game and losing and the loss was so great I would wake up crying. I would feel such grief I would be inconsolable. Games represent the game of life. I had lost the game of life even before I began, and the loss was devastating. I would wake up crying uncontrollably because the loss represented me losing who I was and why I was here. I had rejected my life before I was born, and I was living dead inside. It had to do with my identity and calling in life.

God had to get me to accept my life and who I am. He put His seal of approval on me when He told me this was His world and He put me here. I had every right to be here. It was another life-changing moment.

To have lost myself and my purpose was a loss beyond compare. The grief I felt was overwhelming. To be restored by God and given a second chance, makes me eternally grateful to Him. My last childhood nightmare was solved.

Past Still Exists

I had another experience that really caused me to wonder and realize how strange is the human soul. My husband Jim would never let me tell him my dreams. The topic seemed to upset him. He also told me that he never dreams. I knew this was not so because he frequently talks in his sleep and many times so much that I can tell what he is dreaming about. He will even answer me if I ask him what is going on. The next day I would tell him all he said, and he would have no recollection of his dream.

A few years back Jim had a week when he was talking every night, but what was so strange was his voice. He was talking in a child's voice. I did not think such a child's voice could come out of a grown man. It shocked and amazed me. He sounded just like a little boy and this little boy was mad at the world!

So many times, I have had the desire to know Jim as a child. I wished I could have visited him in that closet he was locked in and told him I loved him. Well, I think I met that child. It was about the third night Jim had been talking in a child's voice and I was intrigued. He had woken me up with his talking, but I couldn't quite make out what he was saying, so I moved a little closer and I said to him gently so as not to wake him up, "What love? "[I often call Jim love.]

"Don't call me love!" An angry child's voice answered, "that's for sissies."

I continued to talk to the boy when I had an idea. I asked him a question.

"Do you know my name?"

"Of course, I know your name!"

Every time he talked, he sounded angry. But the voice was so cute.

"Well, what's my name?"

"Bertha!"

"Bertha?!" I was shocked. We had been married more than thirty years. Why would he call me Bertha?

"My name is not Bertha, "I told him, "It's Summer."

"Summer!" he cried out, "that is the stupidest thing I ever heard of in my life," sounding not only his usual angry but completely disgusted. "Summer is not a name, it's a season."

I was completely shocked and left him alone. I laid there thinking after all these years, I don't care if he is sleeping, he should at least know my name! I never heard that voice come out of him again. That was the last time. But it made me realize how complex we are. I felt like I met Jim as a child, and he was an angry little boy. When I told him about it the next day, he was a clueless as I was.

He had no recollection of a dream or me talking to him. I asked him if there was someone he knew, named Bertha as a child and he said it was their housekeeper.

We are more than we realize. We are complex beings and only God really knows each one of us, we don't even understand ourselves.

But sometimes He gives us a glimpse to what is inside of us through that window to the unseen, our dreams.

Chapter Twelve

How to Respond to a Dream

When You Just Can't Interpret a Dream

There are many times when I just can't interpret a dream. I pray, I look up the symbols and I just don't get it. In fact, that happens a lot. I am going to try explaining one reason I think that happens. And that is we just aren't ready to hear the answer. I have noticed through the years of praying, sometimes I pray, and I get no answer. Then I discovered if I first become willing to do whatever God may say to me, then I will get an answer. It usually takes a great struggle with my will to get to that point. But I have done that before and then I have gotten my answer. It is usually because the answer was not what I wanted to hear and until I became willing to hear it, I couldn't. I will illustrate this point with a hard story.

I had a friend one time; confide in me she thought a close relative of hers was molesting a child. She was in a position that she could have done something about it, but she was confused because she had no proof. The child was handicapped and couldn't speak so there was no way to get confirmation unless she caught this person.

I wanted her to turn the situation over to the authorities because if it was true, I didn't want this child to continue to suffer. My friend's concern was this was too severe of allegations to make without proof. She wanted to pray that God would reveal to her if this was true or not. Well, we prayed, and nothing happened. This made me very uncomfortable.

I really had a pow-wow with God over this. Having had sexual abuse in my own past I am very sensitive about children being abused. I prayed and prayed and prayed for God to reveal this to her.

I felt God's answer to me was this. He knew she could not handle the answer. It would have been a major life change for her to take a stand, and she was not even close to being strong enough to stand up to this person. I felt that if He revealed the situation to her and if she did nothing that in His system of judgement she would have been as guilty as he, the abuser. God would have to punish her, and He did not want to have to do that. She had also been abused all of her life and her life was very overwhelming as it was. God was not going to reveal the truth to her because the end result was that she would fall under judgement.

God handled the situation another way, He took the child home. This situation was severe and God, even God, had no easy answers. I think this is a common situation. God has the correct answer for our situations in our life or even His perfect will, but we are not ready to hear Him. He knows we will not do the right thing, so he hides the answer. It is right there in front of us in a dream that we don't understand.

We have the choice to seek Him and change our hearts and hopefully surrender our wills so we will be ready, and then the interpretation will come. But if not, God would have to hold us responsible for what He was telling us. Perhaps that is why Jesus often spoke in parables.

So, what is the answer?

It is to seek Him, to lay down our will and be ready to be obedient to what He is telling us to do. It may take totally dying to yourself before you will hear what God is saying to you. But if you do, then the answer to the dream or prayer will come.

Prayer

Prayer is the correct response to a dream. If it is a

warning dream then prayer is especially the answer and if the dream calls for some action that needs to change, that warning should be heeded. When my oldest daughter was entering into her early teen years, we had some difficult problems with her. During this time, I had a dream about her in the mall and I did not think it was good. But I had no idea what the dream meant. I just felt it was some kind of warning.

The good news is you don't have to know what the dream means to respond. My younger daughter, who was about eight at the time, was my prayer partner. We entered the dream in prayer. We pictured ourselves in the mall and we prayed. We knew the mall well because my husband worked there for years. So, in our imaginations with the Lord we went in the mall and prayed. We prayed for quite some time until we had peace that the situation had been prayed through.

After we prayed the Lord told me that He was pleased with Joy's prayers for her sister. He wanted to reward her. He told her to go into the Bible Book Store which was in the mall and pick something out. I thought that was the strangest thing I had ever heard of. Because what good does it do to pick something out in your imagination? But Joy did it anyway, she went in and picked out something from Veggie Tales. She loved Veggie Tales.

Not too long after that I was really in the mall and the Bible Book Store had a sign out in front of the store that they were going to have a Very Veggie Party that Saturday to launch the latest Veggie Tale movie which was coming out.

"What a coincidence," I thought to myself. "Could that have something to do with the Lord telling Joy to pick out something from the store?" So, I took Joy to the party that Saturday and they had a coloring contest for the kids. Joy won. She won a Veggie C.D. of the songs from the movies, which was exactly what she wanted.

God rewarded Joy for her prayers for her sister which we prayed for through a dream that we did not quite even understand. But we responded correctly, and God was pleased.

Change

Some dreams call for an action that we must take. Like when I had the warning dream about my patient Myra, I knew I was not to go on the trip she was planning, it would end in disaster. I had to heed the dream.

I had a dream I did not take seriously enough.

I dreamt I needed a hysterectomy but there were two ways I could go about it; one was diet, and one was by surgery.

This dream was calling for me to change my eating habits. I had never eaten right in my life, we ate cheap. I made a half-hearted stab at change but slowly slid back to my old ways and promptly forgot the dream. But in the end, I ended up with a total hysterectomy.

Wait

The last way that I want to talk about how to respond to a dream is to wait. The best example of this is straight from the Bible, in the book of Genesis. My very favorite story in the Bible is the story of Joseph. Joseph had several dreams that meant he would be in some high position. Joseph dreamt *that he and his eleven brothers were binding wheat in the field and his sheave of wheat stood up straight and their sheaves of wheat bowed down to his.*

When he told his brothers the dream, they became angry. Joseph had another dream he also told his family.

He dreamt that the sun and moon and eleven stars bowed down to him.

This time even his father rebuked him, "What is this dream you have dreamed? Shall your mother and I and your brothers come and bow down to you?"

Instead of Joseph's dream coming true just the opposite happened, his jealous brothers sold him into slavery and then they told his father he had been eaten by a wild animal. Joseph became a slave. He served as a slave until his owners' wife falsely accused him and then he was thrown into prison. Things went from bad to worse.

Joseph had received dreams that foretold

greatness in his future but instead his life became horrible, first slavery and then prison. I am sure as he waited for years on end for his deliverance, he remembered his dreams. They must have brought him hope that God had a good plan for his future.

Eventually Joseph's dreams came true. The Pharaoh had a troubling dream that only Joseph could interpret. The Pharaoh's dream foretold seven years of plenty followed by seven years of famine. The Pharaoh was so impressed with Joseph, who had been brought up out of a prison cell to speak to him that he made Joseph the highest ruler in the land, second only to Pharaoh.

Joseph as the ruler of Egypt saved up grain during the seven years of famine. He saved so much it was beyond measure. And then when the famine began the whole world began to come to him for food, and with them were his brothers. The story is told beginning in Genesis 37 and continues to the end of the book.

The point here is that Joseph had to wait for the fulfillment of his dream. And the point is also that Joseph dream did come to pass. Some dreams we have to wait, hang onto and let them give us hope when everything looks hopeless. The correct response to some dreams is simply to wait. God will bring the fulfillment to pass in due time.

Christian Counseling

Sometimes we need some help to respond to a dream. Remember when I opened the door in the back of my closet, the door from the dream. I felt the same fear I had felt my whole life, only much more of it. Too much to handle by myself. I knew what I saw was real, but I did not know how to handle it. I just knew it was too much for me. I just left the situation in God's hands.

Sometime later Jim and I moved to Florida and started going to a wonderful church there. After we moved, God started speaking to me. He said, "You have to do it."

I said, "Do what?"

He didn't answer. A few days later He said it again, "You have to do it."

"What do I have to do?"

He did not answer. He really had my attention because I did not know what He was referring to. I knew He was telling me whatever it was, I had to do, I could not expect Him to do, but what was it I had to do?

The answer came one Tuesday night. Our new church was huge and had many meetings going on. My husband found one on a Tuesday night he wanted to try. It was a deliverance ministry that was affiliated with our new church and used the building. When we got there and sat down, they passed out a program and I opened it. In it I read, **_We have counseling through our office_** and listed a woman counselor's name.

"That is it," God said, as I read it. I did it. I made an appointment. God spoke to the counselor as I walked into the room and told her what happened to me. God opened that door again and this time I faced it with help and with prayer. It was a big step in me getting better.

Sometimes you may need help with your dream. Let God show you who and where.

Chapter Thirteen

Different Concepts

"For My thoughts are not your thoughts, Nor are your ways My ways," says the Lord.

"For as the heavens are higher than the earth, So are My ways higher than your ways, And My thoughts higher than your thoughts" Isaiah 55:8-9

The language of dreams comes from a whole different way of thinking. We have everything upside down. Our way of thinking is natural and belongs to this fallen world. The things that seem real to us are not real. The things that seem so important to us are often times of very little importance on an eternal timeline.

The things we don't think of as real are often times what really is real, like God and the realm of the spirit and dreams. And the things in our life that we are so concerned with are not the things that God is dealing with us about or trying to communicate with us about.

I want a fairy tale life where everything is easy, and I want God to make things that way for me. I want Him to give me lots of money and fix me instantly and fix everyone in my life. I don't want to struggle and even face all the things in me that need changed.

God has different values than I have.

God thinks differently than I think.

God communicates different than I do.

The Spirit Realm is different than our realm.

What I think of reality, isn't reality.

I have to learn to think differently. But it goes even so much deeper than that. My whole reality is off. My reality of God is far off in heaven, and I am way down here on earth, and someday I will get to go live there with Him.

It is all off. It is all wrong, and I have to learn to think totally differently than the way I have thought my whole life.

God is different. Reality is different. What is important is different, and the spirit realm is very different. To think like God thinks and to see things the way they really are bends our minds.

What does this have to do with dreams?

Everything.

Most people dismiss their dreams as nonsense. But the truth is our reality is what is nonsense.

I read something in my favorite book, written by Rick Joyner, called *The Final Quest,* which amazed me. It was about dreaming. *The Final Quest* is a book written from a series of dreams and visions that the author had. In my opinion it is the most important Christian book other than the Bible. I have read it more than fifty times and I never tire of reading it.

I want to quote a portion of the book for you. Rick is having a glorious experience in this portion. He has fought a battle against the enemy as he climbs the Mountain of the Lord. When he reaches the top of the mountain, he finds himself in the Garden of God, and he sees the Tree of Life. The experience is so glorious he never wants to leave but the time comes for him to return to the battle. He is struggling with the idea of leaving. He has a conversation with Wisdom, who is the Lord. The important point I want you to get is what Wisdom says to Rick. I will quote the book.

This was both a wonderful and trying time. Here the "real world" was not real, and the spirit realm was so much more real that I could not imagine going back to the other. I was gripped both with wonder and a terrible fear that I might wake up at any moment and find it was all just a dream.

Wisdom understood what was going on inside of me. *"You are dreaming,"* he said. *"But this dream is more real than what you think of as real. The Father gave men dreams to help them see the door to His dwelling place. He will only dwell in men's hearts, and dreams can be a door*

to your heart, which will lead you to Him. That is why His angels so often appear to men in their dreams. In dreams they can bypass the fallen mind of man and go straight to his heart."

I love this! Rick is dreaming and Wisdom reminds him of this, but his dream is more real than what we think of as real! This is really a different concept, one that upends our way of thinking. Our hearts and our minds are at odds with each other, and we need to bypass our minds. I am glad Rick had these dreams because the book that came from them is amazing and has changed my life!

God is Always Speaking

In this chapter I want to take you even deeper than dreams. You see, God is speaking to you continually. He speaks continually in many different ways; His symbolism is all around us. But let's start to realize God is on a whole different and higher plane that operates totally foreign to the way we think and operate, and His way is so much higher. Not that I have figured out how God thinks, not even close! But I have figured out it is different than the way I think and that my way is wrong, and His way is right. Also, every time I get a glimpse of how He thinks it bends my mind.

My concept of God being far off in heaven is totally wrong! He is everywhere. He is the force that holds all matter together. God is not just around us; we are in Him. God knows everything, absolutely everything including every thought, I think. And God doesn't just speak to us in dreams. His symbolic language is all around us and God is speaking to us constantly in many different ways. Not just to us personally but to all of us. I am going to talk about some of these ways, but they are absolutely mind blowing.

God Speaks Through the Stars

The heavens declare the glory of God; And the firmament shows His handiwork, Day unto day utters speech, and night unto night reveals knowledge. There is no speech nor language where their voice is not heard. Their line has gone out through all the earth, and their words to the end of the world. Psalms 19:1-4

God speaks through the stars. Does that sound taboo like astrology? Astrology is taboo we are not to have anything to do with it, but astrology is just Satan's counterfeit of something very real and powerful. The Bible tells us God speaks through the heavens. God created the stars and the constellations, and He even named them.

He counts the number of the stars; He calls them all by name. Psalms 147:4

In fact, before the Bible was even written the plan of salvation has been written in the stars. The Bible calls the constellations the Mazzaroth. Through the twelve constellations, God had hidden the plan of salvation in plain sight. There are twelve major constellations and for every major constellation there are three minor constellations. I want to give you a very quick rundown of the gospel in the stars. If you study all the stars in each constellation and the minor constellation the complete story is told. It is just amazing.

The constellations begin with Virgo or the virgin. Inside of Virgo are stars which names mean, promised seed, the sent one will come down, the branch, just to name a few. In the first constellation the story of the gospel begins, Jesus will be born of a virgin.

The second sign is Libra, the scales. In Libra we have stars which names mean Redeemer and the wages of sin. The story of salvation continues. The scales represent a legal debt that had to be paid. The scales of justice and mercy had to be balanced through the redeemer.

The third sign is Scorpio which represents death. Jesus faces death and will die.

The fourth sign is Sagittarius, the archer. He stands for the resurrection. His arrow is pointed at a star called Antares which is the heart of Scorpio. He overcomes death. His bow stands for covenant.

The fifth sign is Capricorn, a sea goat. A Goat head with a fish tail. It represents that we, the redeemed, become one with Him.

The sixth sign is Aquarius, the water bearer. It

represents the Holy Spirit being poured out.

The seventh sign is Pisces, two fish tied together. One represents Israel and one the church. It represents His blessed people bringing heaven to earth and greatly multiplied.

The eighth sign is Aries, the ram, He will reign on earth through His people.

The ninth sign Is Taurus, the bull the Messiah will come back with His people.

The tenth sign is Gemini, the twins, in His righteousness we are joint heirs, we will look like Him.

The eleventh sign is Cancer the crab. He will never let us go.

The twelfth sign is Leo, the Lion. He will destroy His enemies.

The gospel has been proclaimed since creation through the stars. But that is just the tip of the iceberg. Each sign and symbol were being played out in the skies in the exact time frame to fulfill the message on earth. Remember the star of Bethlehem that announced the birth of a king!

And there are many more signs in the skies, blood moons and what about solar and lunar eclipses. And they happen precisely when God has planned. How about the total lunar eclipse that darkened the sky for three hours as Jesus hung on the cross?

God is always speaking, and He uses the heavens!!!

Can you bind the cluster of the Pleiades, or loose the belt of Orion? Can you bring out the Mazzaroth in its season? Or can you guide the Great Bear with its cubs? Do you know the ordinances of the heavens? Can you set their dominion over the earth? Job38:31-33

God Speaks Through Nature

For since the creation of the world His invisible attributes are clearly seen, being understood by the things that are made, even His eternal power and Godhead, so that they are without excuse. Romans 1:20

God speaks to us through nature!

Balaam was rebuked by his donkey that spoke to him. The story is in Numbers chapter 22.

God spoke to Jonah through a vine that quickly grew and then a worm ate it. He was teaching Jonah compassion. The story is in Jonah chapter 4.

How about Peter who had just denied Jesus, his heart was pricked when he heard the cock crow.

Everything around us, God is speaking through, both personally, and collectively. He is speaking love; He is speaking redemption and He is speaking divine guidance.

Let's look at some of Jesus words, He was showing us God's messages through nature.

Look at the birds of the air, for they neither sow nor reap nor gather into barns; yet your heavenly Father feeds them. Are you not of more value than they? Matthew 6: 26

So why do you worry about clothing? Consider the lilies of the field, how they grow: they neither toil mor spin; and yet I say to you that even Solomon in all his glory was not arrayed like one of these. Matthew 6:28-29

God's signs are everywhere, to teach us, from the caterpillars who emerge from their tombs with a new life, to rainbows, the seasons, seeds and harvest, our lessons are everywhere.

Have you ever heard of a sand dollar? It is a round flat shell that tells the story of Christ. It has five holes to represent the five wounds of Christ, Two in his hands, two in His feet and one in His side. There is a lily on one side of the sand dollar and a poinsettia on the back and when you break it open inside are five doves, the number of grace.

I used to hold the sand dollar and marvel. I was never able to keep one whole though; I was always compelled to break them open and receive the five doves.

But God speaks to us personally. I remember a Guidepost story I read many years ago. A woman wrote about the death of her father. He had been a farmer and he was born in the same house that he died in. On the day of his birth his parents had planted a tree for him in their yard, which was a tradition back then. Through the years the tree grew huge and shaded their back yard. Shortly after her father died there was a storm and the big tree fell down. She likened it to her father because it was his tree, it represented his life. She missed her father, and she missed the old tree. The next spring, she went out into the yard and what she saw amazed her and filled her with joy. From the stump of the tree five shoots were growing up in its place. Her father had left five grandchildren.

What brings you hope? God is speaking hope, through the symbolism all around you. He is speaking to you daily.

God Speaks Through Events

It is amazing how the events in our headlines are prophetic happenings and are filled with symbolism. Recently just before Super Bowl I saw a prophetic post that Bob Jones had predicted before he died in 2014. Bob said when the Chiefs win the Super Bowl a worldwide revival will soon follow because God is raising up prophetic chiefs.

When I heard this, I did not have a doubt the Chiefs would win because Bob Jones was one of the most accurate prophets of our time. I know absolutely nothing about sports, but my son is a sports fanatic. I called him up and bragged, "I know who's going to win." He said, "I hope

Kansas City."

Those who understand symbolism can find more messages hiding in plain sight, like the number 54. It was Super Bowl 54 the number 54 means seed and door. In other words, a door to harvest. This was a sign!

God is speaking through the events that happen around us. I noticed when Hugh Hefner died was about the time the Me-Too movement came about. It was a throwing off of what he stood for.

The symbolism is all around, look at hurricane Katrina. The hurricane hit dead on in Biloxi Mississippi on the scheduled day of their Day of Decadence, a huge celebration of the gay lifestyle. The name Katrina means pure. Is this a coincidence?

Last summer there were earthquakes in California, they registered 6.4 on the Richter Scale. Isaiah 6:4 says, **And the posts of the door were shaken by the voice of him who cried out and the house was filled with smoke.**

God was speaking through the earthquake that His voice is going forth and causing a shaking. He is always, always speaking. Earthquakes are a sign, there was an earthquake while Jesus hung on the cross.

Or how about Donald Trump's inauguration? His age on the day he was inaugurated was 70 years 7 months and 7 days! What a coincidence!

If we ever had a sign from heaven, it was when we had an eclipse on August 21, 2017. The eclipse was on a path that was 70 miles wide, it entered the US in Oregon the 33rd state and passed twelve states through South Carolina on the 33rd parallel and it was on the 233rd day of the year. The first town it passed through was called Salem, {which is from the word Jerusalem}. It was 99 years since we had a coast-to-coast eclipse, and the last time we had a total eclipse that stayed totally in the US was in 1776. The eclipse is 40 days before Yom Kippur. And seven years from the 2017 eclipse, in 2024 another one will come and cross the nation going the other way and mark a big X across the country.

Do you see any biblical numbers in there? Here is 70, 12, 33 99 and even a very American number 1776. God is definitely sending a symbolic message!

God is speaking to mankind continually.

God is Constantly Speaking

God is constantly speaking to all of us, the believer and the unbeliever. We have to look with a whole new mindset to hear what He is saying around us. God has spoken to me through the numbers on the clock, through billboards, through movies and songs. He is constantly communicating with us. His language is all around us. Here is another example of a marvelous way He spoke to me and brought me hope through symbolism and I was wide awake!

A friend of mine was dying, his name was Ben. He was a quadriplegic and I had been taking care of him for more than two and a half years for five days a week on my job as a home health aide. He and his wife were like family to me. They were both my age so I thought they would be in my life for years to come.

In early September, Ben had gone into the hospital for tests. They, Ben and his wife Patty called me at home and asked me to come up to the hospital. Jim and I raced up there together. Ben told us he had stage four pancreatic cancer. The doctors were not even going to try to treat him, they just sent him home and told him to call hospice.

Ben still seemed pretty healthy so I just could not wrap my head around the fact that he was dying and would no longer be in my life. I was hoping he had a couple more years. I was wrong. Ben went downhill fast.

Ben had become a Christian and loved the Lord, but Ben was not ready to die. Ben loved life even as a quadriplegic. He was on the wild side, especially before he was a Christian, but he was a kind and generous man. Yet, he was not ready to go. He did not have a glimpse of heaven.

He had a rustic home on many acres, that he loved, and a monster truck van that was his pride and joy that he would tear up the road with. He loved his life.

He was really struggling with dying and became

very agitated. He cried out constantly. He wanted something every minute. He wanted to be turned and as soon as he was turned, he wanted to be turned back. Patty, who was not very well herself, could not keep up with him even with helpers coming in.

I know it was hard on her because after a three-hour shift with him I was so exhausted I could not stand it. And he would keep her up all night long. She was falling apart. Hospice decided to put him in a drug induced coma because he was so hysterical, and his wife could no longer keep up the pace.

I realized that night as hospice was there that I would never see Ben awake again. I left his house grief stricken. "This is it," I said to myself, realizing I would never again in this life speak to my friend. I wasn't sure of how I felt about putting him in a coma, but it wasn't up to me. As I drove home that day, I turned the corner onto the same road I always took, it had a tree with a big branch that hung over the road.

I gasped. On the branch was a huge bald eagle. I had not seen one in several years and never this close. But stranger yet was as I was staring at the great eagle who didn't move or fly away, he was staring back. Our eyes were locked.

I knew it was no coincidence. I thought back to my dream of the bald eagle I had several years before and what it meant. It was a sign of death but of a beautiful death of someone entering the Lord's presence.

This was no dream, but I felt the Lord was speaking to me through this bald eagle. But God was not finished, there was more to come. The next day I went to another one of my patients' house. I had been going there also for many years. Her name was Eileen. Eileen lived in the woods at the end of a dirt road that went on until it became a two track. She lived in a little year around cottage on a small lake that had an island in the middle of it. When I arrived at Eileen's she was breathless.

"Oh. It was the most awful thing I ever saw," she cried, and she proceeded to tell me how a deer had tried to cross the ice from the island but had broken through the ice. Helplessly she had watched as the deer had struggled and struggled for life but was unable to get back up on the ice and finally, he drowned.

I could see him out on the ice, most of his body submerged under the broken ice, just the top of his antlers visible. But what made me gasp was what was there next to him, a large bald eagle. All afternoon the eagle never moved but stood guard next to the submerged deer trapped beneath the ice. Then two more eagles joined the one and three bald eagles sat and kept a constant watch on the deer.

I hadn't seen an eagle in years and now in two days I had two eagle encounters, and I knew God was speaking to me in His symbolic language. And it brought me great comfort. What He was saying was this.

Ben was like the deer submerged in the water. He was trapped between two worlds, life and death. He would never wake up again. But God had sent three mighty angels from heaven who were standing guard over him diligently waiting to bring him to heaven. Although I could not see them, I knew mighty angels were watching over Ben and would stay with him.

God spoke to me symbolically through the marvelous world we live in. God cares and He got me out of grief that my dear friend was dying, and he made it real to me that Ben was about to enter heaven and that the angels were there waiting. It is a different concept, but it is real, God speaks to us symbolically through the things around us.

God is always here, and He is always speaking to us. He is speaking in many marvelous ways through our surroundings and our dreams. It is my hope that you will become aware and begin to realize that God is daily speaking to you. He is here in His creation, and nothing exists without Him. He is speaking to you. It takes being aware of Him to hear Him. It is a different concept; it takes a different kind of thinking. Things we think of as real are not as real as things we do not think of as real, like our dreams. God is speaking. Begin to listen to Him in a whole new way.

Chapter Fourteen

Joy's Dreams

My daughter Joy has dreams way beyond the dreams I have had. Her dreams are like adventures in the spirit realm. I have never experienced dreams like hers. I would classify a lot of her dreams as Spiritual Warfare dreams. I will tell you some of them but first I will tell you about Joy.

Joy was saved at an early age. I would say before she was two years old. When Joy was born her older brother, Jamie was six and her older sister, Lonna was three almost four. Both Jamie and Lonna gave their hearts to the Lord when they were three and they both spoke in tongues. When I brought Joy home from the hospital they said, "We can't wait until she is old enough to talk so we can get her saved." They knelt her down and prayed with her so many times when she was tiny, she is not sure when it happened.

Joy had a special dream when she was six years old. We had just moved into our first house and it was a fixer upper. The bedrooms were not finished so the kids, all three and I were sleeping on a queen-sized mattress on the living room floor. I was so thrilled after all those years to finally have my own home that I went to the Bible Book store and bought a picture of Jesus. It was Salman's Christ, my favorite.

Joy was mesmerized by that picture. As we all laid on the floor to go to sleep at night she would lay there and focus on Jesus' face. One night as she gazed at Jesus' picture, she felt a wonderful peace come over her as she fell to sleep. She had a wonderful dream.

Joy found herself outside the city of Jerusalem, she just knew that was where she was. It was light and the colors around her were very vivid. She was standing by an arched stone gateway. Jesus stepped out of the crowd of people and came up to her. He picked her up and set her on a stone wall. She was up on the wall when Jesus faced her and looked into her eyes. His eyes were blue and from His eyes came liquid love which went out from His eyes and into hers. She felt His divine love surging into her. She felt His love fill her; every cell of her body felt full of His love. She was totally saturated in love. Jesus took a piece of bread; it was a flat bread and put it into her mouth. It tasted delightfully sweet as melted in her mouth. At this time Joy woke up and the flavor of the bread was still in her mouth as she woke up.

This was a changing point in Joy's life. The dream was so real it was as if it happened. From that time on she was totally in love with Jesus. She would write Him notes and draw Him pictures, He was her best friend.

When Joy got older, she would often find herself in a demonic realm in her dreams. *An angel appeared to her in her dream and told her she needed to fly away from these places. He told her to fly in the Spirit. Joy noticed that when she flew there was a ceiling, she had to break through to get out of this realm. Sometimes there were false ceilings, and she would have to break through many ceilings. There are demonic creatures in this realm that she encounters.*

One night Joy found herself in this realm and she broke free. She found a workshop that belonged to Satan which she entered and began to look around. On the tables in the workshop there were dioramas set up. They kind of reminded her of little Lego scenes. The Lord told her these dioramas were nightmares. These were what she would be in when she would have to break through the ceilings to escape.

From there she began to fly up to heaven. As she was traveling, she saw what appeared to be cable cars passing back and forth to heaven. The Lord explained to her these were dreams traveling back and forth from heaven to earth. These cable cars were carrying the plans for inventions and solutions to problems in them. {Does this sound strange to you? Many of our modern technology and inventions came to people in their dreams. Einstein's famous theory was inspired by a dream, and another was the sewing machine.

Remember our chapter called different concepts. Things in the spirit realm can seem very strange to us. That is the real world. Joy's dreams are not just dreaming she interacts in the spirit realm.}

Another time in Joy's dreams she broke through the demonic realm and found herself in a class of angels. There was an angelic instructor, and the class was made up of angels. They seemed unaware of her presence. Joy was surprised to find out that the class being taught to the angel students was on her dreams. They were discussing her presence in the demonic realm which often times for Joy were nightmarish.

One student raised their hand and asked, "Why can't we save her?"

"Very good question," the instructor remarked, "Does anyone think they know the answer to that one?"

Another student raised their hand eagerly. "So, she can learn to fight the enemy on her own."

"Yes, very good," the instructor answered and then asked, "Who can tell me how Joy can overcome the enemy?"

Another eager angel raised their hand and when called on replied, "By using scripture."

When Joy woke up, remembering the angel's answer, she decided she needed to memorize some scripture. She wanted to be ready next time she was battling the enemy in her dreams. Joy opened her Bible and found Psalms 144:1 **Praise the Lord my Rock, He trains my hands for war, and my fingers for doing battle.**

Joy did not have long to wait. Once again, she found herself in that demonic realm in her dreams being pursued by evil creatures. As she flew in a circle above them, she remembered her scripture and over and over she said it, **"Praise the Lord my Rock, He trains my hands for war, and my fingers for doing battle. Praise the Lord my Rock, He trains my hands for war, and my fingers for doing battle."**

Over and over, she muttered her verse faster and faster, **"PraisetheLordmyRockHetrainsmyhandsforwar andmyfingersfordoingbattle!"**

As Joy was doing this she looked down at her hands. She gasped in amazement as out of her fingers shot long sharp razors. Every finger became a blade. Joy flew low and she says she ripped those evil beings to shreds with her hands.

You may wonder are these just dreams, what do they have to do with her life?

The answer is no they are not just dreaming, and they do have to do with her life and the world around her. Joy often sees angels and demons in her waking hours too.

Not too long-ago Joy called me after being sent on a twelve-hour midnight shift, to a new patient on her job as a Registered Nurse. The man was on a respirator and needed twenty-four-hour care.

"Mom!" Joy exclaimed over the phone on her drive home from work. "I had the worst night ever, my patient watched the most demonic movie I have ever seen, it was awful, and I had to stay with him. I prayed constantly but demons were manifesting all around me. He has occult things all over the house. I never want to go there again ever!"

"Well thank the Lord you have your new job, and you won't have to go there again," I said. Joy, although working for the same department, was kept busy on a different assignment. The only problem was no one wanted to go there to the new man's house! The patient was verbally abusive to many of the nurses sent there and refused to go back. And even though it meant overtime Joy was scheduled to go there again, this time for three nights in a row.

I was so concerned for many reasons. I had worked midnight shifts for years and they were hard. Especially being tired in a demonic atmosphere which many unbelievers' homes can be. If I would get tired and nod off, I would immediately get attacked by demons. But Joy was working days on top of her midnight shift and this home was especially demonic. It was so demonic Joy could literally see the demons.

The morning of the night she was scheduled to go Joy called. "Mom, I battled the most hideous demons in my dream last night. They used the foulest hideous language and no matter what I was not able to defeat them it was horrible."

"It is the demons from the house you are going to tonight," I said. They are enraged because they do not want you on their territory.

"I know," she said and added "We need to pray."

That night as Joy traveled the long, ninety-minute drive to work there was a terrible snowstorm. Joy prayed in tongues all the way, she shouted in tongues and prayed fervently. I had worked a long day that day but when I got home Joy called. She was stuck in the snow, and she was waiting for a tow truck. "Mom," she exclaimed, I have been praying in tongues and I know what I am saying, the Lord is fighting for me, there is a battle going on." She did not seem the least bit concerned that she was stuck in the snow. Her GPS had turned her down the wrong road that had not been plowed. She said, "Mom I am totally in peace."

Joy waited an hour for the tow truck and when he arrived, he got stuck in the snow also. Joy called me back to tell me. I was thinking she must be miserable, but she was not. She called me periodically, Joy was in supernatural peace, it took four hours for her to get rescued and the bill was over two hundred dollars. But we both knew why she was there, stuck. There was a battle going on over that house and it wasn't over yet.

Joy ended up being four hours late. She got to work at midnight. When she arrived, she said the house was filled with angels. A large angel with a sword appeared to her and told her that the battle was over.

"What was the battle for?" she asked.

"For your peace, "he replied.

Joy wasn't the only one at peace, her patient experienced peace also. So much so he begged her to keep coming back. She talked to him about the Lord, and he responded positively. All three nights were the same. The battle that had started in a dream was won.

Joy has been doing spiritual warfare in her dreams since she was a little child. I do not dream like this. We are all different and God deals with each of us differently.

Chapter Fifteen

Dreams are Spiritual

"And it shall come to pass in the last days," says God, "That I will pour out of My Spirit On all flesh; Your sons and daughters will prophecy. Your young men will see visions, your old men shall dream dreams. Acts 2:17

I want you to get rid of the idea that dreams are just thoughts running around in your head. Although it is possible you may have a dream like that, there is something very spiritual to dreams. There are mysteries to dreams just like there are mysteries to the spirit realm and there are mysteries to everything around us including us.

One time I dreamt that Jesus came back, it was the

rapture! I started to go up, but I got distracted by something I was leaving behind. I started sinking back down, I didn't want to miss Jesus so I started looking up again and up I would go until something back on earth got my attention, I started sinking again. I was going up and down like a yoyo. Then I woke up.

This dream needs no explanation, I know exactly what it means. It was a warning to keep my heart fixed on Jesus, especially when the rapture comes. But that is not why I am telling you this story. A few years after I had this dream, I was reading a Christian book and the author described his dream. It was exactly the same dream I had. The dream about going up and down in the rapture. I was amazed that we had the exact same dream.

God gives some of us the exact same dream! I am not the only one this has happened to. I watched a very interesting video by a pastor who had a very interesting dream.

A pastor named Charles Gallup had an amazing and wonderful dream.

He dreamt he was standing in a field at night, and he was staring up at the beautiful night sky. Behind him he could hear people, he called it the sounds of life. He heard voices and babies crying and a multitude of people and regular voices. As he was watching the sky and looking at the constellations, he saw them start to grow more colorful, it amazed him and he continued to watch the stars actually started moving around out of there constellations, he knew something supernatural was taking place. Then the stars started streaking through the sky and coming to earth. As this was happening, he heard the voices behind him become terrified. He heard sirens and alarms and people crying out in terror. But he felt no terror, only amazement. Soon he started soaring up and as he did, he looked to his side and saw his wife beside him she smiled as they soared together. Soon he burst through a new atmosphere and landed in paradise. He said it was so real. He could smell the flowers and hear the beautiful music. He saw beautiful houses and he wanted to stay there forever. Then he woke up.

He was angry when he woke up because he never wanted to leave that place. He did not tell anyone about the dream for several years because it was such an emotional experience. Finally, he shared the dream with his wife. When he did, she was astounded and said you need to ask your grandson, Parker about his dream.

His grandson had a dream several years before and told no one except his grandmother. So, when Charles sat his grandson down and asked him his dream, his grandson described the same dream. The field, the voices behind him, looking up to the stars, the colors the swirling, all of it the same. Although his grandson saw a little more detail, he was transported to heaven by angels in what he called a cable car and he saw paradise just as his grandfather had.

Charles was amazed that his grandson had the exact same dream he had. He still kept the dream to himself and wondered about it but did not share it publicly.

After several years, Charles was doing a series of meetings out of town and after the meeting a tearful young woman approached him. She told him she had heard the voice of God during the meeting tell her to come and tell him her dream, that he would know what it meant.

Charles immediately felt concern because he had no skills in interpreting dreams, but he told her to go ahead. She began her dream, standing in a field, looking at the night sky, hearing the voices behind her. She described his very dream to him except, when the stars fell, she like the crowd behind her fell down in fear. She never saw paradise. Charles told her the end of the dream and prayed for her to get her heart right with God so she would be ready. It was at this point he started sharing his dream publicly, and I am glad he did. You can see his dream on YouTube.

I find this amazing that different people have the exact same dream. There is more to dreams than we realize. But now I am going to take this one step further. Sometimes there is more than just one person in the dream. Several are the dreamers at the same time! I heard this mind-blowing story on Shekinah worship Centers website, by Joe Sweet. A wonderful church that you can watch online.

Joe tells of an amazing dream. He said he had gotten tired in the middle of the day. That was highly unusual for him, but he got so tired that he left his office and went home and laid down and immediately fell asleep. Joe had an extremely vivid dream.

Joe dreamt he was in a theatre, and he was waiting for a movie to be shown. He saw many in the room he recognized, they were all minsters he knew, and they were milling around waiting for the movie. Joe said he actually felt a strong irritation because the movie wasn't playing, and he wanted it to begin. Joe saw a switch on the wall which would start the movie. He was about to flip the switch when the thought hit him, "I should ask permission from a manager first." Then Joe looked around the room and he saw Bob Jones. Bob Jones was wearing a tag on his shirt which said **Manager.** *Joe caught Bob's attention about flipping the switch on and Bob nodded his head yes. So, Joe flipped the switch and the movie started. Everyone scrambled for a seat. To Joes complete horror the movie was about hell. He saw a huge metal door open up and about sixty people who had just died were pushed into a boiling cesspool. Joe saw the looks of horror on their faces and Joe realized they knew they were damned for eternity. The sight was so horrible Joe was traumatized. He even* *saw someone he knew who had just died. Joe woke up, his heart pounding.*

When Joe woke up and prayed, he heard the Lord say, "I want my people to see Hell because I want them to do something about it."

This dream gets even stranger. Weeks later Joe had a conversation with Bob Jones, on the same day at the same time that Joe was having his dream, Bob Jones was seeing the exact same thing. They were both somewhere else at the same time. The fulfillment of this dream will be the church becoming prepared and doing something about it and stopping people from going to hell.

Joy recently had a dream, and, in the dream, she said to herself, I need to tell mom about this dream so she can put it in her book. Joy felt this was another dream in *the devil's realm, but she did not feel trapped, she was there to learn. The scene of the dream was at a party and a popular boy was there everyone wanted to dance with him, but she was not popular and felt like an outcast.*

"Wait a minute," she said to herself, "this is my dream, I am going to find out what is going on." She started walking around and talking to the different people in the dream. She began asking the different characters in her dream their name.

"I don't know," they would answer her.

"Of course, you don't know," Joy responded, "You are not real."

She realized all these people were just characters, but then something astounded her. She found amongst the characters real people; they knew their names. They were real people also in the same dream at the same time as she was. She was able to easily exit the dream. She felt she was there to learn. Joy told me the dream was very similar to a video game, it was set up the same way. It was coded. Some of the characters were codes and some were real.

Dreams Can Be a Spiritual Experience

What is my point to all of this? Dreams are spiritual. There is so much more to everything than we can possibly realize, including dreams. God has trained Joy for spiritual warfare through her dreams. She is now beginning to see angels and demons with her natural eyes and win her battles with her enemy. Her dreams were her training ground for spiritual warfare. Her dreams and her spiritual life are intertwined.

God has done something supernatural in my life too. He has healed my shattered personality and helped me through my marriage with dreams. My dreams have affected my life in a very powerful way also. Dreams are something very real, they are spiritual.

Chapter Sixteen

A Few Tips on Dreams

You may have noticed that throughout this book, as I have told you my dreams, I have had to give several paragraphs with each dream to explain to you the situation I was in when I had the dream. In order to interpret a dream, you usually have to know a little bit about the dreamer unless your interpretation is actually given to you by God.

My little sisters have called me a couple of times with dreams. They live down in Florida and I live in Michigan I don't see them, so I don't know what is going on when they call. Each time God gave me the interpretation when they asked. This really surprised me because it is rare that God plainly tells me. It has only happened that way a couple of times when I am trying to interpret my own dreams. There are countless dreams I have that I don't know what they mean. Some dreams I don't know what they mean until later, after they happen.

So, my point is that to interpret someone's dream God may tell you plainly or you may have to interview the person and find out what is going on in their lives. I don't even pretend to be a dream interpreter. This book is me just sharing with you, my dear reader, what I have learned through the years about dreams and hoping that I can put you further ahead, quicker in your own experience through what I have learned. So here are some tips.

Write Your Dream Down

It is so important to write your dream down for many reasons.

1. As you are writing you will remember more of the dream
2. Dreams fade quickly, write it so you remember it

3. Some dreams take years to figure out and if they are written down you may be able to interpret it later.

4. The more you write down your dreams and pay attention to your dreams, the more God will speak to you through your dreams.

Always date your dream. Even the date can have a meaning. One of my favorite dreams I ever had a meaning in the date.

I dreamt I was at a train station buying a ticket. I was so excited about the trip I was going on and that I would get to go on this trip with my family. We were traveling by train to a wedding. We were going to a big city. I thought of how fun it would be with my daughters and my sister to be on the train together. I paid the man eight hundred dollars. I went to board the train and it was leaving. I tried to catch the train by running down the track. I was so devastated to miss it. I was angry and crying. I went and begged the man at the desk to stop it somehow. He didn't and told me when the next train would be leaving between 9:20 and 10:20. I went to wait for the next train, I did not want to miss the next one. As I was waiting in the crowd of people for the train, I saw my husband, Jim! I was so happy; I was just overjoyed. I was not going to go alone. A train pulled up on the tracks that looked just like a rollercoaster cart, it was bullet shaped and it seated only two. We got in together and it began to zoom off. As we got going a clear golden shield came down over us and then we shot out at a super speed. I knew we would arrive before the first train. I never felt so happy. Then I woke up.

This was one of those dreams that I did not want to wake up from. It came with such a supernatural feeling. I wanted to be on that train with Jim. When I woke up, I recorded the dream. I knew this dream was about the future, because Jim and I love each other very much but when it comes to who I pray with, it is my daughters and sister. They are my emotional support for everything. Jim appreciates this because he does not want me to talk to him about emotional stuff and he also does not want to pray for hours like us girls do. My daughters and sister and I depend on each other. In the dream I lost that, and I was devastated. Then Jim and I were on a different train built for two.

I knew this dream was telling me the time was coming when God was going to use Jim and I together and it was going to be so wonderful. As of this writing this has not happened yet, and I had this dream years ago. Every once in a while, I would get the dream out and read it again and rejoice in what is coming for Jim and me. Then one time I looked it up again in my dream journal and I gasped when I read the date, I had the dream! I had never noticed it before, it was September 6, our anniversary! God spoke the future of our marriage through a dream on our anniversary.

Symbols in Dreams Can be Exaggerated

Many times, symbols in dreams can be exaggerated. Think of a caricature artist. They take a quality of a person like a big nose and exaggerate it. Dream symbols can be just the same, exaggerated. And there is a very good reason for it.

I dreamt I was riding in the car with a dear friend. The friend, a real person in my life was being suggestive, {sexually} In the dream he hinted, but I got what he meant by it, and it horrified me.

I woke up and thought to myself, "How I could dream that about this person they would never behave that way." I figured the dream was from the devil and dismissed it. Well, later that week the very same person called me and hinted for a favor, to stay over they were coming to town. I agreed but because the situation was so much like my dream, I prayed about it. I was still horrified to have dreamt such a thing about such a nice person.

After I prayed about the dream, I realized what it was all about. I was actually uncomfortable about the favor they asked of me, and I did not even realize it. It was during the height of the corona virus, and they were traveling and wanted to stay at my house, deep down that made me uncomfortable.

The dream exaggerated the uncomfortable feeling because I am not always in contact with my feelings and if the dream hadn't exaggerated the feeling, I would not have dealt with it.

I have noticed this with other dreams also, the symbols are exaggerated.

I dreamt a woman came to my door and lured my husband away. I begged him to ignore her, but he went with her instead, he chose her over me. I was so devastated.

The dream was not about another woman, it was exaggerated. It was a bout with his addiction again which left me feeling like if he loved me, he would not do that.

I remember reading a sort of funny story a Christian book years ago. The author, a pastor *dreamt of a squirrel wearing a pair of glasses that were broken and were held together by a band aid.* That night at church a new woman showed up at his church wearing the exact glasses the squirrel wore with the band-aid and all. She was squirrelly, or in other words a nut. The dream exaggerated the symbolism.

Vivid Colors

Every once in a while, a dream will be very special. It will have vivid colors and you will remember every detail. Dreams with vivid color seem to be from the Lord. Dark dreary dreams would tend to be from the evil one. Some of the most important dreams I have ever had I have never written down; they were so vivid and real I will remember them forever.

Break the Dream Down to the Simplest Form

It can be helpful when you are interpreting a dream that is so full of details to break it down to its simplest form. Remember Lonna's dream we discussed in a previous chapter. We broke the dream down, to a focus and several sub- focuses.

Remember that God wants to Communicate with You through You Dreams

It is God's will to guide you through your dreams. God went to a lot of trouble to get me to finally learn this lesson and I am glad He did. He had a lot of work to do through my dreams and it was His plan to get it done.

Being confident of this very thing, that He who has begun a good work in you will complete it until the day of Jesus Christ. Philippians 1:6

Chapter Seventeen

Dreams from the Enemy

Sometimes dreams can be really bad. The devil takes advantage of any time that we are vulnerable, and we are vulnerable while we sleep. Also, we have to remember Satan is always seeking an open door into our lives. I want to deal deeply with this issue because it is something I have gone through and someone else may also need help in this area.

       We talked earlier in the book about how the Holy Spirit woke me up suddenly and I saw an evil spirit hovering over my face with his eyes boring in on me. I feel this demon's purpose was to oppress people while they sleep. The Holy Spirit woke me up immediately from a deep sleep to reveal this thing to me. It actually seemed afraid when it realized I could see it and immediately disappeared.

Some dreams are from the enemy. I also talked earlier in the book about how other times I felt I was dreaming but it was more like a demonic attack. I will call these night terrors.

I went through many years of Satanic oppression, which I wrote about in my book, *Satan Has No Power Over You*. During this time, my nights were pure horror. I would be fine during the day but as soon as it would start to get dark, I would feel the dread coming on. I suffered from nightmares and night terrors for many years, and I have learned a few things.

My biggest question was, "Why would God allow this to happen to me?" The night terrors were especially horrible because while I was paralyzed, I would feel horrible feelings on my body. It felt like something was slithering through my bones. Sometimes I would be wrestling something. It was beyond awful. It was hellish.

I would wake up and wonder, "Where are my angels? Why aren't they doing their job?"

I remember one day I was reading a devotional and it mentioned a delivering angel. I cried out, "God! You have a delivering angel. I want him send him to me!"

I even told my children all that day God was going to send me an angel that night. And God did. That night the usual demonic attack happened, and I woke up with the sense of evil in the room. But I also sensed the angel I had asked for. He felt like a million volts of electricity. I could sense him by my bed. The evil in the room struggled, then left. I rejoiced thinking that this angel would stay with me for the rest of my life. But he did not. The next night I was back to the same old problems. Why?

I prayed and I rebuked, and I did everything I knew to do. I went through a long battle before I got the victory. Why?

I think back to Joy's dream where she broke through the evil realm and came upon a class of angels. And the angelic class was on her dreams. One angel had asked why they could not rescue Joy. The answer was that Joy had to learn to overcome the devil herself, and she has.

I think this was my answer too, it just took years to understand. You see, from my way of thinking I want my whole life to be easy, a piece of cake. I want to float around on cloud nine and have no problems, ever. I want God to fix everything for me, all the time. But He hasn't. Not that He has left me, although there were a few times I thought He had, but He didn't.

There is something that took me a really long time to figure out. God is making me into His image. It is called training. Training is not easy. I am going to rule and reign with Him someday. He expects me to learn how to overcome evil. This is not pleasant. I do not like evil, it's evil. Yes, I have overcome the night terrors and the nightmares. I have gotten stronger through it all. And yet not too long ago I had some more trouble, more night terrors. I wondered why again.

I realized something else. I was going up a level. I was progressing. I was fighting again.

A Lesson from a Video Game

Years ago, back in the nineties, my son got a PlayStation. I think that is when they were new. My son, Jamie was up on the latest newest video games. To spend time with Him and keep up on his world, I sat and watched him play this thing. Back then the graphics were new and amazing to us.

He had a game where he was on a space station. At first, we did not realize there were many levels. He traveled around through the halls of the space station encountering aliens and trying to kill them. When he finally killed them all we found out that there were more levels. He had to keep moving up levels on this space station. Every time he would conquer a level, he went up this elevator to the next level. Immediately he would have to battle a space alien that was different and harder to beat than the level he was on before. After he would figure out how to beat these new ones then he would be able to move up again. He did this through about thirty levels and then he beat the game and the spaceship launched and the game ended.

I realized I was moving up levels, just like on Jamie's game. I was moving up spiritually and I would have another round with a demonic attack while I was sleeping, and they were tougher to beat.

So how do we overcome the enemy? We pray, we use the word of God and the blood of Jesus and fight. But just like on my son's video game it would sometimes take some time to figure out how to beat the new enemies. Sometimes it takes time and persistence.

I don't like battles with the enemy, but I have to say my whole life has felt like one big battle with the enemy. And every book I have written has come out of what I have learned as I have battled. And every time I have written a book, I have had a battle. So as much as I do not like battles with the enemy, they do seem to be a part of the life of the believer. So, like my son on his video game, let us learn how to beat the enemy on the level we are on and win.

Other Reasons for Bad Dreams

I have found other reasons for having bad dreams are open doors. I have awakened from a bad dream and gone into the living room to find my husband watching movies that I believe caused the problems. The movie opened the door to trouble.

There are some things we have to leave alone, actually a lot of things. They can cause bad dreams. Do not even think about watching a horror movie.

Through the years I have even gotten to the point that I can tell if there is something pornographic or demonic in the house, it will turn up in my dreams. I am spiritually sensitive to evil.

A Bad Dream Come True

About a year or so ago *I had a dream that my grandson was driving the car and he was out of control. I was watching the speedometer and he was going over a hundred miles an hour. I was sitting in the passenger seat terrified I was begging him to slow down.*

I found out from the news that the very same night of my dream, one street over from mine, the police chased a young man they clocked going over a hundred miles an hour. When they caught up with him, he had crashed and his friend in the passenger seat was dead.

I realized I was dreaming about that accident. I don't know why I had the dream, maybe it is a lesson to wake up and pray, maybe God is teaching me something new. I really don't know yet. I am still learning, but I realized I had dreamed about something bad that happened nearby.

Sexual Attacks in Dreams

My daughter Joy wanted me to share her story in this book because she is concerned someone else might be going through what she went through. Joy was attacked by sexual dreams at a very young age. She did not understand why. She suffered for quite some time. She thought that Satan was attacking her for no reason on her part. As she prayed about it the Lord revealed to her what opened the door. She reiterated to me that Satan always looks for an open door.

The Lord showed Joy what the open door was. When she was little, she was playing with the little boy that lived next door. She said he pretended to have sex with a stuffed animal and then told her to do the same thing. She said she felt like it was wrong, but she did it. She realized the dreams began after that happened.

Joy explained to me Satan uses shame to keep us in bondage. She felt ashamed of this memory. The Lord just plainly told her this was the open door, so she could bring it to Him and ask forgiveness. We need never be ashamed to repent before the Lord. It is what brings us freedom. Joy said once she repented, she commanded that spirit to leave her alone and that door was shut from that time on. Joy asked me to tell you that you can shut the door and you can be free.

A large part of deliverance from Satanic bondage has to do with repentance. Even sometimes we have to repent for our ancestors who pass sin down in our family line. It is important to shut these doors on our enemy and keep him out.

Dreams are a good gift from God, but Satan tries to defile and counterfeit everything God does. I have had a fight with Satan in the area of dreams and night terrors. These things have become very rare now, but there was a time I wondered if I would ever get free. God has helped me many times, but He has also had me learn to fight the enemy on my own. We can overcome Satan. God has given us what we need to overcome him.

I recently had a new experience with a bad dream. The dream was hideously perverse. I woke up appalled and wondered how I could have dreamt such a thing. As I prayed, I remembered something that happened the day before. I was walking downtown with my family, and we passed an outside café. The server was a man dressed as a woman. He looked garish. Our eyes met as I passed him. My thoughts were "I can eat anywhere I want. I would never eat there and be waited on by him."

I said nothing out loud and did not think of it again. As I was praying about the hideous dream I had, God brought this young man's face to my mind. But I saw him differently this time. I saw he was in bondage. It was as if there was a demon on him twisting his image of himself and gloating at his appearance with evil glee, the make-up and the frilly clothes. I realized I had responded in judgement, without compassion. As I saw his eyes again in my mind, they looked tormented. I knew the dream was because I had responded poorly. The Lord had wanted me to say a prayer and not pass judgement. I am so glad I had this experience. It taught me a new way to respond. I felt such compassion for him and wanted him free. I pray for him when I think of him. I realize I can no longer pass judgement on people that Satan has bound. I was opened up to that hideous dream by my wrong response. I am glad though because that hideous dream woke me up to my sin, and now I know a better way. Love instead of judgement.

Even attitudes in our hearts can open us up to the enemy. We have to be diligent and careful. Bad dreams can happen for many different reasons. We need to close all doors to the enemy.

Chapter Eighteen

Dreams Are God's Gift

Throughout the Bible are examples of God intervening through dreams. Joseph's ability to interpret a dream for the Pharaoh brought him out of a prison cell and made him royalty. His ability to interpret a dream not only drastically changed his life, but it also put him in a position to save his family and many others from starvation.

Similarly, Daniel in the book of Daniel interpreted a dream for King Nebuchadnezzar. Daniel was also promoted for this. He was put in a high position and was able to use his position for godly influence.

Joseph the earthly father of Jesus was warned in a dream to take Jesus and flee, just before Herod had all the baby boys His age killed! I am so glad Joseph paid attention to his dream.

Dreams and the ability to interpret them are truly a gift from God. But it is not just for those in the Bible, dreams are for all of us.

They show us the deep love and concern God has for each one of us. They save lives, rescue and promote us.

God's Intimate Dream Language

But dreams do even more than that. They show us how much God loves us and thinks about us and how intimately acquainted He is with each and every one of us. God has a language for each of us that is individual and unique, a personal language.

He sees every thought you have; every emotion and memory and He has created a symbolic language to speak personally to you. He speaks to each of us continually. Even using our own thoughts which only He knows, to lead us and guide us.

I am thinking of the dream I had after my parents' divorce. I had thought to myself, "Things will never be alright again." God used that phrase in my dream, it meant something only to me. I knew what it meant; it was His way of telling me my parents would not get back together. He did not want me to have false hope.

I realized how well; He knows me. He heard my thoughts. He is in the world that is inside of me, a world of thoughts and emotions, a world of my conscious mind and my subconscious mind. Only God really knows me. I don't even know myself!

The Window to the Unseen

Dreams serve so many purposes. They truly are a window to the unseen. They show what is inside, they reveal secrets and things that need to be healed. My childhood dreams were a window to the trouble within me. They helped me to deal with the underlying problems and showed me what I needed. They show us our own situation from a higher perspective and show us things we cannot even admit to ourselves.

But dreams are so much more than that! They show us the future, they warn us of things to come so we can pray ahead of time. They can warn us of the enemy's plans or show us if we are on the wrong path.

We receive answers in our dreams. We receive guidance in our dreams, and yet so much more. Remember Joy, my daughter, she saw the carts coming from heaven with ideas and inventions. Other's dreams have affected everyone's lives. Much of our technology we all enjoy had come to their inventors through dreams.

God is intimately involved in each one of our lives, and one of the ways He communicates with us is through our dreams.

God has done impossible things in my life. When my husband and I were married almost forty years ago, everyone knew we would never make it. Many people told me years later, "We did not think you would make it; we did not know why you married Jim."

I was a mess and Jim was a mess. Jim could not stay out of trouble for long and I was so far out of reality that I had no hope for a normal life either. We had no hope on our own. And even with God things seemed hopeless for us many times. But God gave us miracle after miracle.

I was so broken that I could not even take someone disagreeing with me about anything. I would get dizzy, and the room would spin. Yet, I lived through many years with an alcoholic husband who screamed for hours at night. How did I survive?

God got me to see my real enemy, he taught me through my dreams and gave me a different perspective. I saw my real enemies were four invisible giants that were oppressing my husband. I saw I needed to love and forgive my husband to defeat my real enemies. My dreams were God's gifts to me. Gifts of guidance and gifts of wisdom, gifts of perspective, and knowing I was not alone. He was with me, and He was not ever going to leave me. God showed me a different picture of my husband. A man who would not stop fighting, no matter what, even though it seemed he could never win. Jim's motivation to keep fighting was love. Love for God, love for me and love for our children,

I found out other things from my dreams, why I could not function in this world, and what was wrong with me. But God did not leave me broken. My past still exists, but my past has been healed. I no longer have dreams of the door in the back of the closet because that door has been opened and what was in there has been dealt with and healed. I know longer dream of the lady in the safari suit because I have been put back together, I can live now. And I no longer dream of playing a game and suffering such loss that I can't stop crying. God has my life now; He holds all my cards in His hands.

And I don't cry every night anymore. I have stopped beating up myself. I did not know how beautiful my spirit was to Him. I look like a little girl full of sweetness to Him. His dreams have given me so much.

God set me on the path of life, and He used my dreams to help me find it and keep me there. We can all step on that path, and no matter how much we have against us that path will lead us right through it. And best of all we don't travel that path alone, God has promised us that He would go with us.

I have a prayer for you, my readers. That your window to the unseen will open and you will see how much God loves you. That He will answer the question to your past that still exists, and He will heal your hurts and you will begin to experience miracles, one at a time, as He speaks to you, and guides you, and heals you through your dreams.

I love you all, sweet dreams,

Love, Summer

Volume 3

Dictionary of Symbols

I wanted to give you a dictionary of symbols with a word of caution to go with it. God has created a language personal to you that only you will understand. Each house you have lived in may appear, or something that only He knows about, a thought you had or a pet or a toy. So, my dictionary may or may not help you. The dictionaries helped me because so many times when I had no clue what I was dreaming about, and I learned a lot from dream dictionaries. This dream dictionary is going to be different than others because I have used what different symbols have meant to me. Remember to ask yourself questions and remember you won't know what every dream means, but you can still pray about every one.

A. Numbers

1 God, beginning, first

2 witness, testimony, multiplication

3 Trinity, complete, resurrection

4 seasons, creation, world

5 grace, favor, five-fold ministry

6 man, labor,

7 perfection, completeness

8 new beginning, Jesus

9 fruitfulness

10 trial, test, law

11 late hour, disorder, confusion

12 apostolic, fullness, divine government, discipleship

13 rebellion, sin, backsliding, my birthday

14 double anointing, Passover

33 Jesus' age

40 trials, testing

100 fullness, hundred-fold return {Isaac had a hundred-fold return on his crops}

666 mark of the beast

1000 millennial reign

B. Colors

Black: Sin, death, famine

Blue: spiritual, heavenly, revelation, depressed, baby boy

Brown: earthly, imperfect

Gray: Uncertainty hazy, [gray area] old or mature

Green: peace [green pastures} life, growth, new or unlearned

Orange: danger, caution, warning

Pink: flesh, new growth, baby girl, feminine

Purple: royalty, kingly, luxurious

Red: sin, blood of Jesus, passion, wrath of God

White: purity, righteous believers

Yellow: hope

C. People

Artist: skill, beauty, seer, prophetic

Athlete: one who competes, running the race of life

Baby: something new, a new thing being birthed in your life

Birth: bringing forth something new

Dentist: pastor, leader, he represents understanding or your ability chew on something

Doctor: The Lord, wisdom, an expert in health

Family: real family, spiritual family, church

Farmer: Preacher, pastor, Christ

Father: God, spiritual covering, mentor, natural father {my dad stands for action in my dreams, because he is a go-getter}

Husband: natural husband, Jesus

Judge: God, authority

Mother: the church, heavenly Jerusalem, nurturer, actual mother, my beliefs

Miscarriage: death of something you were to do or an idea

Names: names have meaning, look up the name in a name dictionary

Nurse: caring person, Jesus, the Holy Spirit, an angel

Policeman: authority, God, Jesus, angels, it could be you exercising authority, or challenging your own decisions

Wife: actual wife, church

Animals

Alligator: large mouthed enemy, dangerous person

Beaver: industrious, hard worker

Butterfly: having a metamorphosis, a change, new life, coming to maturity and beauty

Cow: wealth, cash, blessing

Deer: longing for God, dear, peaceful

Dinosaur: something huge, something old, something overwhelming

Dog: best friend, comforting friend, {good} demonic attack, {bad}

Dove: The Holy Spirit, innocent

Elephant: big issue, powerful, large

Horse: strength,

Lamb: Jesus is the lamb of God, we are His sheep

Lion: Jesus, Satan

Owl: wisdom, demon

Ox: strength

Racoon: rascally behavior

Sparrow: not insignificant to the Lord, provision

Wolf: enemy, vicious {in one of my dreams it meant generational curse}

E. Buildings and Places

Airports: change of ministry, or location, waiting on the Holy Spirit, spiritual refueling

Amusement Park: fun, enjoying life

Attic: subconscious

Back door or porch or yard: from the past

Bakery: making spiritual food for others

Bank: your heart

Barn: church, storehouse

Beach: boundary, boundary of heaven and earth

Bed: intimacy, peace, covenant

Bridge: crossing from one place to another, connecting, the cross, Jesus

Building: the church, a business,

Church: your spiritual life, may be a certain congregation

Closet: past, stored memories, hidden self, quiet place of prayer

Court: a trying time, judgement

Door: a new opportunity, a portal, entering or exiting a situation

Elevator: going up or down, moving quickly to a new level

Fence: barrier, boundary, protection

Field: the world, harvest, the church

Front porch: the future

Garden: intimate place with the Lord

House: self, body, emotional house, past house may refer to childhood or whatever was significant about the house, days of your life, people

Hospital: church, place of healing

Hotel: many different compartments of the personality

Kitchen: heart, place of preparation

Mall: place with many choices

Mountain: God {in the mountain], meeting place with God [on the mountain}, obstacle[mountain in front of you]

Ocean: humanity, many people, depths of God

Pool: small gathering of people, spiritual refreshment

River: movement of God, Flow of the spirit {dirty water} flesh and spirit

Roof: covering, protection, authority

Room: chambers of the heart

School: time of learning or training, church

Window: vision, {front window} vision for future, persons eyes

F. Vehicles

Ambulance: emergency, need immediate help

Bicycle: situation in life or ministry that requires much effort

Brakes: needing to slow down or stop, ability to stop

Bus: crowd, {church bus} church or ministry {school bus} learning time

Car: life, moving through life, {new car} new way of life, {car breakdown} trouble, hindrance to life

Driving: moving through life, {speeding} careless living, {highway} moving rapidly

Flat Tire: hindrance to going forward

Gasoline: fuel, refilled, spiritual filling with the Holy Spirit

Gas Station: place to receive filling, spiritual powerhouse

Highway: path of the righteous, clear path, spiritual progress

Motorcycle: personal ministry, going alone

Moving Van: change, a move

Plane: soaring in the spirit, taking a higher way

Road: journey of life, {bumpy} troubles in life {city streets with curbs} regimented life

Road Sign: direction for life

Ship: large ministry {cruise ship} worldly church

Truck: work

G. Weather

Autumn: end, completion, time to work

Blizzard: hard time, loss of sight, adversity

Clouds: God's presence, change coming, the saints

Flood: mighty move of God, satanic move, great sin

Ice: cold, lack of love, frozen plans

Lightning: supernatural power

Rain: revival, Holy Spirit falling, favor, refreshing

Rainbow: covenant, promise, hope

Tornado: great adversity, spiritual warfare

Sky: what is coming on the earth, {depending on the sky, blue sky} peace {dark sky} trouble {winds} change

Snow: purity, cleansed from sin

Sun: father, life giving, favor

H. Miscellaneous

Arm: strength, influence

Antiques: memories, past experiences

Badge: authority

Barking: enemy 's intimidation

Bathing: cleansing

Belt: the belt of truth

Blanket: covering, authority, love or covering mistakes

Bricks: human made empire, rebellion against God

Bread: the body of Christ, the word of God

Bread and Butter: provision

Camera: memories, focusing, catching a moment

Cell Phone-Phone: communication with God, when I get a phone call in a dream the message is very important, when I can't get through on the phone, usually dialing 911, spiritual opposition to my prayers

Change {coins]: favor, small changes

Check: prosperity, finances, provision

Clothes: deals with attitude of heart, garment of praise {good} spirit of heaviness {Bad}

Coma: unresponsive, loss of conscience spiritually asleep, inability to respond

Cup: human vessel, portion, communion

Desk: learning, business

Dust: human, confusion, contempt [Shaking the dust from your feet}

Electricity: power of God

Electric Wires: fear of man {In Joy's flying dreams if she could not fly higher than the power lines it represents fear of man}

Falling: loss of support, loss of income, emotional let down

Flowers: expression of love, heavenly, beauty

Fountain: source of life, Holy Spirit flowing, monument of blessing

Games: wasting time, fooling around, distraction, fun, the game of life

Gifts: blessing, spiritual gift

Keys: authority over the enemy, opportunity, access to enter

Kissing: agreement

Lamp: the word of God, a believer, truth

Luggage: weight from the past, burdens, traveling, ready to go

Mailbox: message, expecting a message, human heart

Map: seeking direction, guidance, the Bible,

Mirror: vanity, focus on self, the human heart, seeing clearly,

Money: talents, provision, God's favor, spiritual or natural wealth

Newspaper: Current events, the gospel, publishing

Ring: covenant, authority, sign of wealth

Rock: Jesus, refuge, strength

Salt: preservative, adds value, purifies, seasons

Shoes: [on] prepared for ministry, equipped ready [off] worshipping on holy ground, ill prepared, {new}: new calling, {boots} spiritual warfare {high heels} seduction [slippers] comfortable, rest

Swimming: moving in spiritual gifts, moving through life

Teeth: understanding, able to chew or understand, [broken teeth] unable to chew, could also refer to words being spoken

Television: a vision, prophetic vision

Vacuum Cleaner: cleaning, deep cleaning, getting something ready or cleaned up, deliverance

Water: [clean} the Word of God, the Holy Spirit, pure speech, purity [dirty} impure, strife, sin

Watch: watch out, be careful or keep watch, having to do with timing

Epilogue

I wanted to end this book with an opportunity for those of you who have never given your life to the Lord to do so. A door is open to you right now. The door is the beginning of a new life. I went through that door when I was fourteen years old.

It was so simple. Jesus told me He loved me, and I told Him I wanted Him. When Jesus told me, He loved me He meant it. I have spent a life in His love. His love is so incredible I have no way to explain it to you. But I want to encourage you to give yourself totally to Him. Will you pray with me?

Jesus, I need You, please come into my heart and take all of me. I want to live for You.

Notes

Chapter 13   The Final Quest by Rick Joyner

www.morningstarministries.org page 44

www.ingramcontent.com/pod-product-compliance
Lightning Source LLC
LaVergne TN
LVHW011227080426
835509LV00005B/367